COACHING
CHAMPIONS

SOCCER COACHING IN ITALY

An in-depth analysis of the world's most successful soccer coaching system, based on interviews with:

- ♦ Italy's World Cup-winning coach Marcello Lippi
- ♦ the coaches of Italy U21s and Women's U19s
- ♦ coaches from top clubs like Juventus and Inter Milan
- ♦ experts from the FIGC, the Italian soccer federation

by Frank Dunne

**Library of Congress
Cataloging - in - Publication Data**

Coaching Champions:
Soccer Coaching in Italy
by Frank Dunne

ISBN-13: 978-1-59164-113-1
ISBN-10: 1-59164-113-6
Library of Congress Control Number: 2008927256
© Frank Dunne, 2008

Art Direction, Layout and Proofing
Bryan R. Beaver

All Photographs
© Frank Dunne, 2008

Printed by
Data Reproductions
Auburn, Michigan

Reedswain Publishing
562 Ridge Road
Spring City, PA 19475
www. reedswain.com
info@reedswain.com

This book is dedicated to the memory of my father, Michael, and my mother, Margaret.

Introduction

World champions! On 9 July 2006, Italy won the World Cup final in Germany. It was the fourth time that the Azzurri had lifted the trophy, placing Italy just behind Brazil among soccer's superpowers.

After a nail-biting penalty shoot-out with France, Italy captain Fabio Cannavaro lifted the famous gold trophy in Berlin's Olympic Stadium. Cannavaro and his team mates that night – Buffon, Zambrotta, Grosso, Materazzi, Gattuso, Pirlo, De Rossi, Camoranesi, Perrotta, Totti, Del Piero, Toni and Iaquinta – will be forever idolized by their nation.

The exploits of the team and its coach, Marcello Lippi, will be analyzed by soccer coaches and students of the game around the world, keen to understand the mechanisms and psychology of peak performance, of winning when it matters most. To do so they will need to look beyond June-July, 2006, and even beyond the 18-month qualification cycle.

The foundations of Italy's World Cup success go much deeper and can be found in the country's highly successful coaching system. In October 2006, at Coverciano, the technical center of the Italian soccer federation, Lippi told me: "You don't win a World Cup for any single reason. There are many factors but the starting point is having a group of players with excellent values. The technical-tactical evolution of the players comes through their development in the youth set-ups in Italy. A national team is not like a club where you have players from many different countries and soccer cultures. These are Italian players. They are products of the Italian soccer movement, which is an important movement, one which is highly evolved tactically. There are excellent coaches at every level right throughout the system starting from youth football. So when players arrive at the national team they are at a very high level."

Winning the World Cup is a clear sign of the health of a country's soccer, but there is another important measure of the strength of Italy's soccer system – the success of the U21s. Having won five of the last nine editions of the European Championship at U21 level, Italy undoubtedly has a strong claim to being Europe's most successful breeding ground for young players.

At the heart of the Italian coaching system lies the federation's technical center at Coverciano. It is here that aspiring coaches, mostly ex-professional players, are given the kind of grounding in the theory of coaching which has led many coaches to describe it as a kind of "university" of soccer.

Italy's World Cup success is not the only recent evidence that Coverciano produces top-level coaches. In December 2007, the Football Association of England appointed an Italian – Fabio Capello – as head coach, charged with leading England to the World Cup finals in South Africa in 2010. This was followed in February 2008 by the appointment of legendary Italian coach Giovanni Trapattoni to the national team of Ireland. At club level too, Italian coaches are in demand around the world.

The Italian system produces great coaches who, in turn, help to develop great players. These players are dedicated to their profession, highly capable technically, with high fitness levels. Most of all, they have a tactical flexibility which prepares them for almost any match situation. When Marcello Lippi claims that "Italian players are the best in the world tactically," who can argue?

What gives Italy the edge? What ideas and methods are used during that 10-12 year journey which turns a promising child into a top professional? How do coaches balance work on technique and ball skills with work on team tactics? At what age should winning become important? How is work on fitness and strength integrated into the coaching?

Coaching Champions attempts to provide an insight into how players are coached in Italy from the moment they first join a soccer club through to their participation in major championships at U21 level.

Coaching Champions deals primarily with coaching in a professional environment where young players are groomed to compete at the highest level. So it provides professional coaches from around the world an opportunity to compare their own approach and methodology with that of Italian coaches.

Hopefully, the ideas it contains will also be stimulating and useful for coaches at amateur and grass-roots level, whether they are qualified coaches, school teachers with a passion for the game or parents who are lending a helping hand. It includes nearly 50 easy-to-follow coaching drills, from basic passing and receiving exercises through to complex attacking moves. These are not theoretical "blackboard" exercises but are drawn from actual coaching sessions and are explained by the coaches themselves.

I hope that this book will also be interesting to the average soccer fan – at least to the kind of fan who thinks a little about the game.

Bologna,
March 2008

CONTENTS

Part 1

The Azzurri: World champions

Marcello Lippi on winning the 2006 World Cup:

"You have to be able to impose your personality on the group without nullifying theirs."

Marcello Lippi occupies a unique place in the pantheon of great soccer coaches: he is the only coach to have won both a World Cup and the Champions League/European Cup. The former Juventus coach was appointed as Italy's commissario tecnico in July 2004, after the disappointing results of former Italy coach, Giovanni Trapattoni. Lippi gave the team a clear identity and a style of play which was reminiscent of his Champions League-winning Juventus team of the mid-90s.

Italy qualified for the World Cup with 23 points from a group containing Scotland, Norway, Belarus, Slovenia and Moldova but it was the performances of the team in two friendly games which really alerted the soccer world to Italy's true potential. In November, at the Amsterdam Arena, Italy comprehensively outplayed Marco van Basten's Holland in a 3-1 win – the first defeat for Van Basten as Holland coach. This was followed in March by a 4-1 demolition of Juergen Klinsmann's Germany in Florence.

Just before the World Cup began, AC Milan player Alessandro Nesta, one of the pillars of Italy's defense, explained the key to the transformation which had taken place between 2004 and 2006: "What Marcello Lippi has given to the national team more than anything else is enthusiasm and a belief in our own abilities. We were a bit down [after Euro 2004] and he lifted us up again. Afterwards, he started to spell out his tactical ideas but his most important job was the one he did on our heads."

Lippi himself began to notice that a group spirit was being forged after one particularly fierce league match between Juventus and AC Milan. The following day, the Italy squad got together and the same players who the night before were bitter rivals, were now enjoying themselves around the dinner table. "If you see players disappearing off to their rooms or to their mobile phones, it's not a good sign. That day they were happy to be together, chatting and laughing. A good bond had been created."

Lippi's 4-3-3

Much of Lippi's success in Germany was down the team's solid defensive qualities. Italy conceded only two goals – an own goal and a penalty. But Lippi has never been a negative coach. He enjoyed success at Juventus with a 4-3-3 formation, which relied on the three forwards – usually Alessandro Del Piero, Gianluca Vialli, and Fabrizio Ravanelli – working incredibly hard to press the opposing defense high up the pitch when the opponents had possession.

With Italy too, Lippi showed a fondness for 4-3-3, but, as he pointed out, when talking to a group of soccer coaches in Bologna, he is not wedded to any single formation: "The most stupid thing that a coach at any level can do is to try to

3

impose a specific formation on a group of players, regardless of the characteristics of those players. The tactical approach always has to be determined by the players you have at your disposal."

Lippi's version of 4-3-3 is different from the classic Dutch interpretation of the formation, which works best with two natural wide players. Lippi prefers two center-forwards, who operate fairly close together, and one player operating just behind, either 'in the hole' or in a wide position, ready to come inside and link up with the other two.

Lippi's strikers, Fiorentina's Luca Toni and AC Milan's Alberto Gilardino, are strong enough to operate as target men, holding up the ball with their backs to goal, but are also highly technical. This gives the team the opportunity to put together short passing moves in the final third, without pushing too many midfield players forward, and also to play longer balls from deep.

As Lippi explained: "Our starting point is the knowledge that we have a fantastic goalkeeper [Gianluigi Buffon], a defense which is envied by everyone, and quality midfielders. I also started with the idea of always using two strikers. Lots of national teams have good forwards but many have problems at the back. Two strong forwards, who are good with their feet and in the air, are going to cause problems."

Lippi argues that the limited time available to national team coaches means that the defense and midfield can only reach a "reasonable" degree of tactical organization, not the kind of automated, almost unconscious harmonic movements that endless of hours of repetition on the practice pitch, week in week out, can give club sides. As a consequence, he says, success at national-team level has increasingly become dependent on having players who can produce something special or unpredictable in the final third.

Lippi also believes firmly in continuity. While England coach Sven-Goran Eriksson, for example, astonished everyone by selecting the 17-year-old Theo Walcott – a player yet to make his Premier League debut – Lippi made no surprise choices, picked no player who had just run into a last-minute spell of form. The coach made it clear that he saw the trip to Germany as the final part of a project which had lasted 18 months. "Why should I ruin the work of a year and a half? Over two seasons you understand the contribution that everyone can make, not just in technical terms but in terms of collaboration, conviction, participation and seriousness".

Youth coaching

After retiring as a player, Lippi became coach of Sampdoria's U20 Primavera team in the 1984-1985 season. "It was a natural move for a player at the end of his career to go into youth coaching and as I had spent 16 years as a player at Sampdoria, the club was the natural choice. Coaching youth soccer should not be the choice of someone who can't find a first-team job somewhere else. It has to be a mission. Whoever does it has to be profoundly disposed towards doing it, has to be prepared to give everything. You have to get the idea out of your head about becoming a big football manager when you're coaching young players. After three years, I realized that it wasn't for me. I wanted the risks and the tension of the battle in the league table, of defending your city's colors."

"My advice to coaches of elite young players is to work on perfecting technique, to focus on the continuing improvement of the individual player. This is where you need the ex-professionals who have the patience to work with kids on their skills. The kind of work you do obviously depends on the age group. You're not going to do the same activities with U13s and U15s that you do with the U20s. With the younger kids you should leave tactics out of it completely. Young kids should be taught how to play in every area of the pitch, not taught to play a specific role. They don't need to be taught a role because it is innate. Every player has a natural disposition towards one role or another but first they have to learn how to play everywhere."

"At U20 level, the players are 18 and 19 and ready to start working like adults. However, one of the big mistakes in soccer is that when a young player breaks through to the first team, coaches stop working on his individual technical development and he is coached as a team player. There is a risk that if young players get promoted too soon in that kind of environment, their technical development will be arrested. Every coach should decide for himself the right amount of time to spend on coaching team tactics at this level but it shouldn't take up most of the training time."

The long road

After the Sampdoria U20s, Lippi became first-team coach at Pontedera (Serie C2, the fourth division), then, in subsequent seasons, at Siena (C1), Pistoiese (C2) and Carrarese (C1). Lippi then had two seasons in Serie A with Cesena followed by a season in Serie B with Lucchese. He then had one season in Serie A with Atalanta and one with Napoli before his big break – taking the helm at Juventus in 1994.

"My coaching career has been made up of a series of steps. I have coached from Serie C2 right through to top Serie A sides and the national team. You learn something at every level, it's a constant growth. But you have to have the desire to learn, to know more and to exchange opinions with people."

5

"When I was 25 and still a player I decided to do a coaching course. I wanted to understand what was happening in the game and in training. Coaches never really explained why they were doing things. I took the Category 3 coaching badge and it really opened my eyes. I started to understand about fitness preparation, about tactics and things like sports medicine. I realized then that I would be happy to be a coach one day."

"When players stop playing and move into coaching they think they already know everything but it's not true. After the first three months as a coach I was doing things that had never entered my head before and three months later I was doing things that would never have occurred to me in the first three months. I kept on learning. A coach has to always consider that his knowledge of the game is insufficient and to continue to find ways of expanding it."

Practical experience

Although Lippi encourages a constant craving for knowledge, he warns against putting too much faith in coaching theory. Real knowledge must be gained first hand. "You won't find the answers in books or going to watch other coaches run training sessions. Knowledge has to come from accumulated experience. You could go to watch Louis van Gaal or Jose Mourinho running a session. But what they are doing on that day relates to their specific needs with that group of players in that moment. You could read manuals and simply copy the exercises but do they have anything to do with your team? I prefer to go home after a training session and invent five or six exercises that are based precisely on what my team needs."

"You need to accumulate a well of knowledge to know how to adapt to things. You could plan a training session and find on the day that the weather conditions aren't right for it. Or you could spend time preparing a particular exercise and then pick up at the training ground that the players aren't in the right place psychologically for that exercise. So you have to be able to adapt and change things around."

Coaching the national team

"If you ask any coach who has been in soccer a long time they will give you the same answer: the quality of the players is the most important factor in a team. You need players with good technique. Where teams are evenly balanced in technical terms, other factors come into play like character, knowledge and personality. As the national team coach you have to pick the best players, not those who you think will be able to adapt to your ideas. Then you have to learn to play in two or three different ways, which means working a lot in training. In some countries, like England, every club plays in the same way, which makes it easier for a national team coach. In Italy, every club plays with a different tactical approach. Juventus play with one formation, Palermo with another, Milan with another again."

"The real job for a top coach nowadays is managing men. These days you have players who have earned enough in one or two seasons to resolve all of their problems for life. It's not so much about teaching them how to pressurize the opponent, how to play the offside trap and so on, although you have to do those things. It's about having the right personality. You don't have to be nice and you don't have to be nasty. <u>You have to be able to impose your own personality on the group without nullifying theirs.</u> You have to make the players feel that you are a strong guide but also that you are making use of what they know and what they can do."

"To win a tournament, you need motivation, a special group spirit. My Italy team was already a strong group but when the Italian soccer scandal erupted [in May 2006] they knew how to transform everything that was going on into positive energy. This wouldn't have happened if the group hadn't already been convinced of its own strengths."

Winning the World Cup: group spirit and tactical flexibility

Group Stage
Italy 2 – 0 Ghana
Lippi began the tournament with the 4-3-1-2 formation which he had used many times in qualification, with Francesco Totti returning from injury to start 'in the hole' behind two strikers, Luca Toni and Alberto Gilardino. A lapse of concentration by Ghana's defense allowed Andrea Pirlo to pick up a short pass from a corner and score from the edge of the box. In the second half, Totti was replaced on 56 minutes by Mauro Camoranesi as Italy switched to a more conventional 4-4-2 to make it harder for Ghana to break them down.

Despite having only 47 per cent of possession to Ghana's 53 per cent, Italy managed 13 shots on target to Ghana's four. The low shots-on-target figure for Ghana is a tribute to the level of Italy's organization in the non-possession phase. Despite being under pressure for long periods, Italy only conceded eight free kicks to Ghana's 22. This kind of discipline has two benefits: fewer players get suspended and the opposition gets fewer opportunities to use set plays.

Italy 1 – 1 USA
Lippi confirmed the same starting 11 with the same formation but the game did not go according to plan because of three red cards, two for the USA and one for Italy. The first half finished 1-1 and the bulk of the second half – around 43 minutes – was played 10v9. Italy dominated possession with 54 per cent to the

USA's 46 per cent but as both teams tired, neither was prepared to take risks. Italy had only three shots on target in the whole game, the USA had zero (the USA goal was an own goal by Italy defender Cristian Zaccardo).

Italy 2 – 0 Czech Republic

A point would have been good enough to send Italy through so the priority for Lippi was not to lose the game, who switched to a 4-4-1-1, or 4-5-1, formation with Totti playing off a single striker, Gilardino. The game was finely balanced for long periods but was tipped crucially in Italy's favor early in the second half when the Czechs had Jan Polak sent off. Even playing 11v10 for over 40 minutes, Italy had only marginally more possession (52:48), and fewer shots on goal (6:8). Italy were defending a one-goal lead and hoping for a counter attack. Lippi sent on Filippo Inzaghi for Gilardino with half an hour remaining and it was Inzaghi who broke the Czech offside trap in the 87th minute to score the second.

"For the first time in ages I moved away from playing with three attacking players. We knew that if we beat the Czechs we would top the group and avoid Brazil. The Czechs play with one striker and lots of midfield players. So I went with one striker and lots of midfield players. Why give them the advantage? However, goals arise out of specific situations. So I can't say that our goals were the product of the tactical formation."

Last 16
Italy 1 – 0 Australia

On paper, Lippi appeared to have selected an attacking formation, reverting to 4-3-1-2, with Alessandro Del Piero replacing Totti behind two strikers, Toni and Gilardino. It was soon clear, though, that Italy were sitting deep, conceding territory and looking to mount counter attacks.

 This may have been Lippi's tribute to his rival coach Guus Hiddink, whose teams are always aggressive, well-organized and never stop running. In the afternoon heat, if Italy had taken on Australia in a physical battle, they might have struggled. Lippi opted for a tactical battle, the kind of battle in which Italian players are well versed. Australia finished the game having had 59 per cent of possession (they played with an extra man for 40 minutes) but only managed four shots on target to Italy's six.

Quarter final
Italy 3 – 0 Ukraine

Lippi again started with the apparently more cautious 4-4-1-1 formation, with Totti playing off Toni. However, Italy attacked Ukraine from the outset at a high pace, with Lippi suspecting that the weakness of the Ukraine side lay in the defense. This strategy paid off in the sixth minute with Italy full back Gianluca Zambrotta scoring from distance.

The Ukraine reorganized after the early shock and started to come back into the game, dominating Italy for long periods of time. Incredibly, given the final 3-0 score line, the Ukraine had 59 per cent of possession to Italy's 41. As in previous games, the advantage in possession terms did not translate into a material advantage, with both teams having seven shots on target.

Semi final
Italy 2 – 0 Germany (aet)
In a finely-balanced match, with two teams committed to attacking, Lippi took the crucial initiative as the match appeared destined for penalties. He sent on two attacking substitutes, finishing the game with four forwards: Totti, Del Piero, Gilardino and Vincenzo Iaquinta.

"I realized that the game was no longer being played in midfield. It was a case of Italy attacking, then Germany attacking, then Italy attacking. The forwards and the defenders of each team were those doing the work. Seeing as we have a very strong defense – far, far stronger than Germany's – I said: let's put on four attackers and go for it. It meant that we were ready with the right players to take penalties if necessary. But we had good luck."

Final
Italy 1 – 1 France (5-3 on penalties)
Italy and France both lined up with a 4-2-3-1 formation. Having had one extra day to recover from the semi-final, Italy were expected to be fresher than France but the demands of the semi-final had taken a heavy physical and mental toll on Lippi's players.

Italy had the advantage in possession terms (55:45) but France made better use of the ball, creating five strikes on goal to Italy's three. As tiredness crept into the game in the second half, neither side appeared willing to push extra players forward to break the deadlock. Penalties loomed and Zinedine Zidane's red card for butting Marco Materazzi cost France its best penalty-taker.

"We had a good first half but the players were tired after the semi-final and in the second half France's better technique and organization began to tell." After 61 minutes, Lippi made two changes: playmaker Francesco Totti and midfielder Simone Perrotta were replaced by the aggressive midfielder Daniele De Rossi and striker Iaquinta. "Putting in De Rossi helped beef up the midfield and Iaquinta started to stretch them. After that, the game became very finely balanced again. We didn't create many chances but France didn't pose us any great problems."

Part 2

The Azzurrini and Azzurrine

Italy's U21s and Women's U19s

Preparing for major tournaments

Chapter 1

The U21s prepare for the 2007 European Championship in the Netherlands, with Pierluigi Casiraghi and Gianfranco Zola

"We share a vision of soccer: it must be beautiful to watch"

After Italy's elimination from the U21 European Championship in Portugal in 2006, the Italian soccer federation decided not to renew the contract of coach Claudio Gentile. The decision was something of a surprise, given that Gentile had led Italy to victory in Germany in 2004.

Former Lazio, Juventus and Chelsea forward Pierluigi Casiraghi was appointed as team coach. Gianfranco Zola, who played with Napoli and Parma in Italy and achieved legendary status in England during his time with Chelsea, was made technical consultant. Roberto Dujany was retained as fitness coach, while Italy U16 and U17 coach Antonio Rocca, and former Napoli keeper, Luciano Castellini, were brought into the coaching staff.

Casiraghi, Zola and Castellini were speaking at Coverciano, the federation's technical center in Florence, as the team prepared for 2007 tournament.

Pierluigi Casiraghi, team coach:
Gianfranco and I have the same vision of soccer. We prefer a style of soccer which is as beautiful as possible. We want to play soccer in the true sense of the word. We want to play as many talented players together in the team as possible. It doesn't always work like that in Italy. Here, the tactical formation often takes priority over the players. In the national team, I think that it's better to play the best players. That might sound simple but it's not. Playing as many of the most talented players as possible gives us, as coaches, great satisfaction and I think that the players enjoy themselves more too.

It's not easy to find the right balance between this vision of soccer and the need to win games. In Italy, the result is usually the most important thing. Gianfranco and I have spent time in England – me for a short while, but

Gianfranco for many years – and it was a very formative experience. One thing that it taught us both was that the result is not everything. We think that this is the right approach, especially with younger players.

We're in a very finely balanced group. It's probably tougher than the other group. England have an excellent team, even without [the injured] Theo Walcott. They have got real quality and nearly all of them play in the Premier League. So they have to be one of the favorites to get to the final. Serbia are always very difficult to play against. The current team is strange because they can play a brilliant game and then play badly. They're hard to figure out. The Czechs are the strongest team physically in the whole tournament. It will be difficult. We want to win it, but so do the other seven teams.

In Italy, we probably work more than any other country on tactics during our training sessions and players do this from a very early age – too early, in my opinion. But our players grow up with knowledge of all the different tactical systems. They can play with a back four, a back three or whatever. So it's not complicated for a new coach to come in and change the tactical approach. They have the flexibility to adapt not just to a change of coach but even to a change of tactics during a single match. Tactically, you always have to be able to adapt to the characteristics of the team you are playing against.

Today was our first real pre-tournament training session so we started to work from the base, which is always the defense. In the coming days, we'll carry on with the rest of the team.

Training session 5 June 2007

5.00   Players arrive, some begin to warm up by passing a ball around, others begin a light jog

5.25   Team talk with all of the coaching staff

5.27   The keepers split off and begin work with Castellini; the other players begin a jog around the pitch. Then there are a couple of minutes of stretching

5.30   10v10 match in small pitch, three poles for goal posts; the pitch continues for 10m behind the poles so that goals can be scored from behind the goal as well in front. Mostly played with two and three touches on the ball. (Diagram 1)

15 mins

5.45   Stretching, posture work, running progression 2 x 20m

14

Italy's U21s in a warm-up match in training in preparation for the 2007 European Championship

5.48   Speed resistance work. A diamond with players split into groups by colors. A relay between the four bases, each about 25-30m apart, players pass a bib to team-mate

6.00   10v10 match, three-touch, in small space. Offside rule applies. A goal is scored when the ball is carried over the end line after a through ball by a team-mate

6.15   Players split into two groups. Casiraghi takes defenders and some midfield players; Zola takes attackers and attacking midfield players

Casiraghi: Situational exercise 5v4 and 6v5, with keeper. The point of the exercise is organizing the back four, keeping the line at the right height and with the right distances between the players. The attacking players try to switch the ball rapidly from side to side, looking for a run through the defense which enables a through ball (Diagram 2)

Zola: Shooting practice from edge of box. One-two with Zola then shot from edge of box. Then Zola moves out wide. A ball played wide, a cross by Zola for a shot on the full, first time

6.30   11v11 match in half-sized pitch

7.00   Ends

Roberto Dujany, fitness coach:
Every training session is characterized by two methods. One is the called 'the cocktail method', the other is called the 'sandwich method'. The cocktail method is used to improve the metabolic qualities which a player needs: the central and peripheral components, the ability to rapidly build up lactates.

15

The term 'cocktail' refers to the fact that the metabolic qualities – such as strength, speed and stamina, or rather aerobic capacity – are mixed into the kind of athletic activity which is required of the player. According to the type of work proposed, one of these can predominate, just as is the case during agonistic performance. It's vital that the work carried out is of a high quality and therefore is conducted at high intensity.

'Sandwich' means splitting fitness exercises between periods of ball possession activities, or technical-tactical activities. We use a combination of activities with and without the ball. Today we used one activity without the ball, which was the one dedicated to resistance to speed.

There are also activities which don't have a direct energetic utility but which are designed for the prevention of injuries, the development of physical sensitivity and recovery from the stress produced by intensive sporting activity and physical traumas.

These activities are only an indirect part of fitness preparation but are equally important because of their preventive aspect, especially when you bear in mind that the players are at the end of a long season. These activities include: work on mobility of the joints; postural gymnastics; a rebalancing of the tensions from the stretching of the muscles; proprioceptive gymnastics; gymnastics for the feet muscles; gymnastics to help wind down the entire structure through movement of the coxofemoral, of the lumbar column, and the pelvis; and gymnastics for improving the stability of the torso.

This year we have a higher number of players who were heavily involved in the championship race both in Serie A and in Serie B compared to last year. So they have given much more on a physical and mental level and we had to take that into consideration when planning the training and the preparation in general. Around six or seven players have been involved in the Serie B run-in, which has not yet finished, and they joined us late.

The other problem was the overlap of the game against Albania on Friday for qualification for the 2009 U21 tournament in which four or five of our players were involved, one of whom then had to go straight away to play in Serie B. We started here without all the players and with several players who were tired. So at the outset we decided to reduce the workload a little in training.

The work we do during the year is always linked to what the players do in their clubs. Their main job is to play for their clubs. We have good relationships with our colleagues at the clubs, with the coaches and the doctors, to monitor how the players are getting on physically. There is a high element of personalized work. We always work in a group because the group is very important in

16

soccer, as in all team sports. Within the group, I divide them into sub-groups and then within the sub-groups everyone's work is to some extent personalized according to the rhythms they are used to working with in their own clubs. It's a very detailed approach.

I wouldn't like to make any big claims but the group looks in good form to me ahead of the tournament. Today there was a good spirit out there. Yesterday, all we did was a bit of warming down and this morning they did nothing, so this is the first real training session. This was the first time that everybody was together, which probably contributed to the relaxed atmosphere.

Luciano Castellini, goalkeeping coach:

The most important thing in my work is dialogue with the keepers to know what kind of work they have done during the year. Our work with them is very marginal and we can't alter the equilibrium they have. It's all about collaboration. I give them advice and they usually accept it but I also get them to explain to me what they need. It's pointless proposing something which could do more harm than good.

In tournaments usually only one keeper out of three gets to play. But it's easy to manage this situation from a psychological point of view because they know more or less how things will go. The keepers on the bench know that in modern soccer a keeper could easily get sent off by getting his timing wrong by a fraction when coming out for the ball, so they can never sit quietly on the bench. They have to support the team and always be ready for action.

The work of a goalkeeping coach has not changed that radically during the years, regardless of changes in laws like the back-pass rule. My theory is that, when kicking, the keeper should play safe and when in doubt kick it long rather than risk making a mistake. In modern soccer there is nearly always a fine balance between teams and one goal could cost you the match.

Communicating with the back four has always been a vital component of a keeper's make-up. But they grow up with that. It's probably true that you require a particular character to play in goal if you consider that every day you are throwing yourself on the ground but people choose the role because it's what they enjoy. Nobody has made them become a keeper.

These days there are no secrets in soccer – the players all know each other but at this level there are often changes in the line-ups, with new players coming in. We study our opponents on video, looking at set plays, who are the dangerous players, who has a good shot and so on.

Our players are tired after a long season but a change of environment always gives players a boost and wearing the national team shirt is a good motivation. This is a stepping stone to the full national side so they play and train with passion. The success of the U21s in the past does add some pressure and tournaments can be a lottery but they are good players and they are used to playing at a high level.

Gianfranco Zola, technical consultant:
The fact that Gigi [Casiraghi] and I have had the experience of playing in England helps us, not just with regards knowing the England players we are going to come up against but also with understanding their mentality, their approach to playing. This is a big advantage.

In this Italy U21 group there are many players who hold down regular places in top teams and this is partly down to a change in Italian soccer where there is a greater willingness among the big clubs to give young players a chance but it is also true that this is a very talented bunch of players.

There has been a general reduction in the basic technical level of players across the board. Once, there was more time available for kids for motor activity, now even young kids have loads of things on the go and they don't dedicate that much time to motor activities.

Technically and tactically I'm not sure that a coach can make that much of a difference at this level with the time which is available. We rely a lot on the ability of our players. We can give them the benefit of our experience to help them through certain situations. That's what we hope. We'll have a good idea of whether or not that is the case at the end of the tournament.

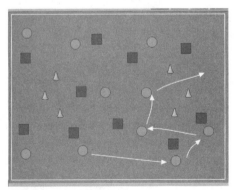

(Diagram 1) 10v10 warm-up match

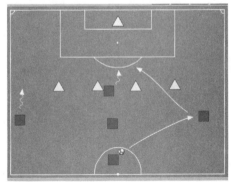

(Diagram 2) Situational exercise for the back four

European Championship 2007

Group Stage
Italy 0 – 1 Serbia
Italy 2 – 2 England
Italy 3 – 1 Czech Republic

Italy came third in the group, behind Serbia and England, and were eliminated.

Chapter 2

The U21s prepare for the 2006 European Championship in Portugal, with Claudio Gentile

"A relaxation of motivation levels cannot exist"

Claudio Gentile, a World Cup winner as a player with Italy in 1982, coached Italy's U21s to victory in the 2004 European Championship in Germany – the fifth victory for the country in seven editions of the championship. Despite being courted by many top Italian clubs, Gentile stayed on to lead the U21 team to the 2006 European Championship finals in Portugal by winning a qualifying group which included Scotland, Moldova, Slovenia and Belarus, before beating Hungary in a play-off match.

Claudio Gentile

Gentile was speaking at Italy's training camp in Pescara, on the Adriatic coast, just days before the squad headed off to Portugal.

Motivation

Any Italian player selected to represent the country at U21 level knows he has big boots to fill, given the record of success of Italy's U21s. Such a track record could easily become a source of pressure for the players but Gentile didn't believe that this was the case with the 2006 squad. "The last group of U21s which I coached, which won in Bochum, also knew that there was a great tradition to respect. I think that it worked as a motivation rather than being a source of fear that they might not be able to achieve the right result. This was demonstrated by the fact they we lost the first match and then went on to win all the others. It was a stimulus, not a pressure that would prevent them from playing the way they know how to."

The coach also rejected any suggestion that his own motivation levels might drop, having already won the event. "It's not in my nature. In my career, I have won a lot. The experience of winning pushes you even harder because you want to always achieve something prestigious – something that you can put in your trophy cabinet, as they say. So for me there is no question of a lack of motivation, quite the opposite. I am used to this. I played at a great club [Juventus] and for a great national team where such a relaxation of motivation levels could not exist."

"Many things can influence you along the road but the hunger to do well must be inside you from the beginning. I always had that. From the earliest age, I was determined to make it as a soccer player, even when people told me that I had no chance. Then I went to Juventus, a club with a winning mentality. At Juventus, when you win a game it is forgotten immediately and you are already thinking ahead to the next game."

"If a coach has had a successful career as a player it's easier to win the respect of young players. If you have a certain image, an authority, what you say gets through immediately, which might not be the case with someone who has won nothing. But it's also important for a coach to know when to say nothing. There are many coaches who react to adversity by talking too much, by telling players where they have made mistakes and this can sow confusion among young players. After we lost to Belarus, in the first game of the European Championship in 2004, I told the players that any team can lose one match and that it was important to remain united and not to worry about criticism from outside. From there, the team really took off."

"In Germany in 2004, I was able to call upon my experience of having played in the World Cup. I recalled the things that, as a player, I had thought were positive and I tried to apply them. In 1982, we started very badly and we got a lot of criticism, so when the U21s lost the first game I was able to say, 'I've lived this situation as a player and I know that if we remain united we can still win.'"

Tactics

To some extent Italy was heading into uncharted territory with its 2006 group-stage opponents. "Denmark and the Ukraine are taking part for the first time and Holland haven't qualified for a very long time. So there will be certainly something new. There will be new talents from every country who will emerge. I expect that technically it will be a very high-quality tournament."

Given the challenge presented by unfamiliar teams and line-ups, being able to adapt tactically during matches would be vital. With this group of players, Gentile had a preference for 4-4-2 but he explained the importance of being able to react to what other teams are doing: "Our tactical approach depends very much on who we are playing and can change a lot from opponent to opponent. It depends how they play: do they play with a single striker? With two trequartisti [the creative player behind the forwards] or with one? You have to know how to adapt to every formation presented by the opposition otherwise you end up with players that are of no use in the context of the team. If the opponents are playing with a lone striker and I have four defenders, at least one of them can be sacrificed, so you can push that defender forward into the midfield. You have to always be ready and prepared to change. You can't afford to be presented with a tactical situation which your team doesn't know or a tactical solution which they are trying out for the first time."

"We watch videos of our opponents. We study our opponents, we look for what areas of the team are strongest, who are the key players, the ones who dictate the play, the leader, the one who wants the ball. Everything is studied carefully to allow us to make the necessary counter moves. Of all of the skills a coach must have, reading the game is absolutely fundamental. It's the way for a coach to take on and beat the opponent. Everything has to be planned to render your opponents less dangerous and to try to create as many difficulties for them as possible during the game."

"We are here in Pescara for a week and have no more than 10 days together before the beginning of the competition. The choice for a coach has to always be for the player who can give you something extra, who can finish off the work of the team. If you have this kind of player, you have a better chance of winning. In this U21 team, we have players like Giampaolo Pazzini and Raffaele Palladino, who are both very good technically and who also good finishers. We build around them a style of play which suits their strengths. If one is good in the air, we try to look for ways to provide him with opportunities to make use of that quality. If another is better with the ball on the ground with rapid interchanges of short passes we also study this type of solution."

Man-marking and zonal defending

Most Italian clubs have used zonal marking in open play for the last 15 or 20 years. At set-plays, some teams use man-marking, some use zonal marking, and most use a combination of both. Gentile was probably the greatest man-marker in the history of Italian soccer, so it's not surprising that he should try to use his expertise with the U21s. His team uses a combination of zonal marking and man-marking in open play which is unusual in modern Italian football and requires a lot of work.

"We work a lot on the defensive phase, both in open play and on set plays. In open play, from the moment the opponent crosses the half-way line, certain mechanisms are triggered which must prevent the other team scoring. There are moments when we have to switch from zonal marking to man-marking and we are good at this. But it requires continuous work and preparation. This group was created two years ago, so if a new player comes in to take the place of another he already knows how to perform his role."

"I don't think that it's harder to man-mark these days than it used to be, just because of the new interpretation on tackles from behind. First of all, I think that the rule preventing fouls from behind is absolutely right and should have been in place a long time ago. The player doesn't have to make a tackle from behind. He can hold up his opponent through his positioning. The crucial thing is not to give your opponent time to turn and take you on directly. If you can apply this kind of pressure without making a tackle, it's already positive. Trying to anticipate your opponent, to intercept the ball, is something which has to be only attempted in a situation of absolute safety. I always tell players that it is better to hold up the opponent rather than risk intercepting the ball because if you get it wrong and make contact with the opponent you can pick up a red card."

Gentile's man-marking skills were crucial to Italy's 1982 World Cup victory. He stopped two of the world's best players – Maradona and Zico – from hurting Italy. He explained how he had prepared. "Before the match against Argentina, I studied Maradona for two days on videotape. I looked at his strengths and weaknesses, if you can use the word weaknesses when talking about Maradona. I came to the conclusion that the secret was not to let him turn. If he could turn and run at you, he was gone and you would never catch him. They were very different kinds of players. Maradona was a soloist; he could destroy a team with individual skill. Zico did it by playing off his team mates."

Observation
"I observe the fitness training sessions with a very specific objective. From these exercises, I can see which player is moving quickly, who is a bit more mechanical in his movements, because maybe he is a bit more tired than the others. If my presence can help to motivate the players, then that's a positive. But I'm always looking at the players and what they are doing, how they perform at speed and in tight movements, to see what kind of condition they are in. For me, this kind of observation has always been fundamental."

18 May 2006 Training session, with fitness coach Roberto Dujany
The U21s spent one week training at the seaside resort of Montesilvano, near Pescara on Italy's Adriatic coast. The location was chosen because its climatic conditions would be similar to those of northern Portugal, where the team would be based during the European Championship. Between Monday, May 15 and

Friday, May 20 the team had 10 training sessions, two per day, with fitness work in the morning and technical-tactical sessions in the afternoon. Fitness coach Roberto Dujany explained the objectives of one of the morning sessions.

Warm-up

10.10   A light jog, lasting around 4-5 minutes, covering 1.5 laps of pitch. "This is a typical start to the session just to get things moving."

10.15   A series of stretches, 10-15 seconds maximum for each, with no repetitions, lasting three minutes. "This is just a minimum of mobility work for upper and lower limbs."

10.18   A circuit, lasting 12 minutes, with players divided into four groups of four to five players, spending three minutes on each area. Using two circles of plastic markers, one group of five players plays head tennis, the other juggles the ball with the feet. Four players, two stationed at one end of the circuit and two at the other, about 30m apart, hit long balls to each other. In the middle of the area is a smaller circuit made of various items of equipment: "wobble pads" (stability balance balls), hoops, poles, hurdles and plastic discs.

"This is still part of the warm-up but is now more specific because it requires a certain type of attention at the level of the motor senses, so it's not just about warming up the muscles but is also work for the brain, which is important. The attention required, the concentration, is the kind which is characteristic of the player who needs to be ready automatically from when he hears the first whistle of the referee. He has to be ready, has to be in the right condition to enter immediately and fully into the match."

"In the central circuit, with the various bits of equipment, the players choose their own activities, deciding what is most appropriate for them. They are arriving from various clubs and will have different training habits, so each player has two to three minutes to work on something specific to him. Those who used the wobble pads a lot, for example, were working on their proprioceptive sense."

"We always work in a single group but within the group there are sub-groups at work, and within these sub-groups every player has his own personal rhythm, according to his characteristics and habits. They are all top-level professional players – three are from Serie B, all the others play in Serie A – but there are those who have played a large number of matches and those who have played fewer."

Speed and reactivity

10.30 For 10 minutes the players embark on a series of exercises based around sprinting short distances at maximum speed, which are interspersed with more spells of short stretching, primarily on the lower limbs. The exercises include:
- a sprint, forwards and back, with knees brought up high
- a sprint with a change of direction, right or left
- the players are divided into two lines, one opposite the other, and sprint at full pace with an intense skip over low hurdles; the first time, the player turns and returns to his own line, the second time he continues moving forward to the other line
- a similar activity with a sprint in and out of hoops

10.40 For 10 minutes the players make a series of short, intense sprints from various starting positions, interspersed with short spells of stretching.
- players lie down, face to the ground, with hands on buttocks, on the whistle, they get up quickly and sprint for 3-4 meters
- a sprint at the whistle starting from a kneeling position
- lying with the back on the ground, getting up and sprinting
- lying with back to the ground, making a sit-up movement and then, on the whistle, getting up fully and sprinting

Finally, the players sprint forward about five meters to a cone, at which point they turn at right angles and run backwards as quickly as possible for about five meters.

"This phase of the session is all about speed and reactivity. The second part, in particular, is about reactivity, with the reference point being the whistle. The players were told not to look at me but to react only to the audio signal. It's about being ready to react immediately to certain signals on the pitch."

Box-to-box runs

10.50 The players are divided into three groups, about 80m apart (at the edge of each penalty box) and take turns to run the distance at a medium pace with a regular stride, for a total of eight minutes. Only one groups runs at a time, with two resting.

"I divided the players into groups according to their aerobic capacity. Again, within the groups, each player works according to his own personal rhythm. It's a slightly boring element but we are preparing for a major tournament at the end of a long season and this kind of activity serves as a general regeneration for the players and also provides the players with the basis to help them recuperate between matches, in which recovery periods are very short, and also to recuperate within the game itself."

Injury prevention

11.05 The players lie on mats and conduct a series of stretches for around 10 minutes. Some players leave after 10 minutes, others continue. The stretches include:

- lie down in press-up position, raise one leg behind the body, then the other, four times for each leg
- lie on back, push up the pelvic area, three repetitions of 10 pushes
- sit-ups with one knee coming up towards the chest, then the other
- lying on back, rotating leg in a wide arc, first right then left
- lying on back, right ankle rests on left knee, rotate legs, then change legs

"This is work designed to help prevent injuries. We place great importance on stretching, posture and mobilization of the joints, especially the pelvic area – the coxofemoral – where there is, in my opinion, a kind of crossroads at a muscular level which is crucial for the soccer player. I also consider this to be a kind of healthy form of gymnastics which is helpful for the soccer player but which is often

overlooked. I understand that there is always less time for coaches but I believe that conducting a proper activity designed to prevent injuries is fundamental for the wellbeing of athletes."

"We didn't conduct tests on the players prior to the training. In the last two or three days we have been able to make an assessment of their fitness levels in training and also in their performance in the technical and tactical work which Gentile has been doing in the afternoons. In the afternoons they rest in their rooms and at night they go to bed around 10pm or 10.30pm. They look after themselves in this regard. After dinner they go for a short walk and then go to bed. They are tired at this point, after a day's training."

European Championship 2006

Group stage
Italy 3 v Denmark 3
Italy (4-4-2) took the lead after 16 minutes but Denmark (4-2-3-1) then scored three times before half time. Italy pulled two goals back in the second half, including one in the 90th minute.

Gentile: "The players showed incredible character. After we scored the first goal, the team became stretched and they stopped pressing but at half time I said to the boys, 'all of Italy is watching, it's time to play with some pride.'"

Italy 1 v Ukraine 0
Italy (4-4-2) needed to win, the Ukraine (5-3-2) only needed to draw, having defeated Holland in the first game. The Ukraine man-marked Italy's two center forwards, Rolando Bianchi and Raffaele Palladino, and doubled up on Italy's wide players, Pasquale Foggia and Alessandro Rosina, allowing Italy few opportunities to penetrate the Ukraine back line. One lapse of concentration by the Ukraine in the 92nd minute allowed Italy defender Giorgio Chiellini to score from a header inside the box.

Gentile: "It was very difficult to play against the Ukraine. They were only interested in stopping us playing and created nothing going forward. It wasn't easy to get past the wall they put up but we showed again that this team never gives up and we deserved the victory."

Italy 0 v Holland 1
Italy (4-4-2) needed only a point to qualify whereas Holland (4-1-3-2) needed to win. Italy played a game of containment but gave away a sloppy goal after 74 minutes which was enough to put them out of the tournament. Holland went on to win the final 3-0 against the Ukraine.

Gentile: "It was right to allow Holland possession and try to close down the space. If we had been under pressure for 90 minutes I would be critical of my approach but we were only punished by a single episode. I would choose the same team again and would ask them to do the same things. If I had played with just one striker, the press would have lynched me. If we had attacked Holland and conceded a goal on the counter attack, they would have said I was mad."

"This squad does not have less quality or personality than the squad which won the European Championship two years ago but in that group, 15 of the 22 players were regular first-team members. In this group, there are only three."

Chapter 3

The Women's U19s prepare for qualification for the 2006 European Championship, with Corrado Corradini

"Women players are more sincere and less crafty than men"

Italy's Women's U19 team was aiming to take part in the 2006 European Championship in Switzerland in July. If the team qualified, the tournament would mark a highly successful end to the first year's work of new head coach, Corrado Corradini, one of the most experienced coaches of the Italian soccer federation, who took over the team in July 2005.

Corrado Corradini

In March 2006, in preparation for the second-phase qualifiers in Slovakia, Corradini took the team to play in the La Manga tournament in Spain, which involved Italy, Norway, France and Sweden. Prior to the tournament, Corradini gathered the team for a two-day training session, described below, at the La Borghesiana sports complex in Rome.

First steps: July 2005 to March 2006

"We carried out selection trials last summer to choose the squad to take to the first-phase qualifiers of the European Championship in Israel last September. When I was appointed, I had very little experience of women's soccer but I have found it a wonderful experience. This is a marvelous bunch of girls who helped me from the outset."

"Of the group of 20 girls, only eight play in the top division, Serie A. Most play in the second division and there is a big difference between the demands of the two divisions. The rhythm and intensity of the matches is completely different and it is immediately noticeable in the levels of the players. Far fewer girls play soccer in Italy than in the north of Europe, especially Scandinavia, so teenage girls here grow up without that soccer culture. One consequence of this is that they are not as aggressive as girls who are used to playing from an early age. They are easily put out of their stride by a push or a shove or by someone pulling their shirt."

Getting to know the players
"With limited time, it's not easy to get to know the players well. We see them once every 30-40 days and stay together for no more than two to three days. The longest time together so far was in Israel, where we started to get to know each other. Getting to know women players is less complicated than getting to know male players. Women are more sincere than men, in my experience. They are less crafty. I have developed a fantastic relationship with the girls. My approach is probably lighter and more relaxed than with men's teams, precisely because it's a man-woman relationship. I'm extremely sincere with them and they understand that everything we do, we do for their good. I'm like a father to them."

"I'm tougher with men, who are more likely to take liberties and look for short cuts. With women, if I didn't call a stop to the training session they would just carry on forever. Men are also more presumptuous. Nowadays, you have boys of 18 and 19 on stratospheric money – they feel like champions of the world and it's hard to get them into the culture of hard work and self-sacrifice. I had big arguments with one of the boys of the U20 team last year in the World Championship. He felt that he was already a top player and couldn't be told anything but he was a player who had a lot to learn."

First-phase qualifiers
In Israel, Italy notched up three victories: 15-0 against Armenia, 3-0 against Austria and 1-0 against the hosts. "What impressed me most about my team in Israel was their technique. I had imagined that it would be a long way behind that of men's soccer but I noticed that there were some girls who were really good technically. The other positive thing I noticed – and this is what made me fall in love with women's soccer – was that women players have a genuine propensity for hard work, application and seriousness in training."

"We believe that this is a good team but they weren't fully stretched in the first phase. Armenia weren't really on the same level at all – it was just a group of girls thrown together. Austria and Israel were also of a lower level technically. Having said that, Israel made life difficult for us. It was very hard to score against them and, being at home, they had quite a passionate crowd behind them. My girls aren't used to playing in front of big crowds so there was a psychological pressure that they found a bit difficult to deal with."

"Since then, we have been closely monitoring women's soccer throughout the country. We played a friendly at Malta in February against the Malta Women's first team and won 2-0 – an excellent result. Compared with the teams from northern Europe, though, we are some way behind physically. There is a stamina deficit because there are no leagues in Italy which can compare with those in northern Europe. The La Manga tournament is our first opportunity to really see what this group is capable of."

Training Session, 9 March 2006

Pre-session meeting: 3pm

The team is set to depart for Spain on Saturday morning. First, there are two days of training, Thursday and Friday. Before the Thursday session, Corradini calls a meeting to outline his hopes for the tournament and to stress one key tactical point: movement off the ball. Using a white board, he sketches out some typical movements, showing how when the ball goes forward, the whole team has to move accordingly, with the defense pushing up. In the attacking phase, he stresses, it is the timing of runs off the ball which create the space for goal-scoring opportunities: "the player that 'makes' the pass, is not the player in possession but the player who makes the run. The run is what dictates the type of pass, where it goes, how hard it's played and so on."

Training session: 4pm-5.30pm

"We designed the training session bearing in mind that the girls have come from a week's hard stamina and strength work with their clubs so if we load them up with more heavy physical work, there is a risk that they will get injured. So there is a light warm-up, some technique work, shots on goal and a match. The goalkeeping coach wasn't available today so rather than leave the keepers on their own doing very little, I spent a lot of time shooting so that they were fully involved in the session and enjoyed themselves."

Warm-up: 15 minutes

All the players line up on the half way line, each with a ball. The players run with the ball at a slow pace to the edge of the penalty area and then return to the half way line. The ball is carried out with the right foot and back with the left. The players then repeat the course, bouncing the ball ahead of them as in basketball, right hand out, left hand back. The run is repeated with the ball being passed from hand to hand at around head height. Then the players run with the ball again, alternating between carrying it with the inside of the foot and the outside of the foot, as if preparing to dribble an opponent, feinting left and right with the upper body. The players then move laterally, dragging the ball along with the sole of the foot. After each run there is a one-minute break for stretching, mostly of the leg muscles.

"It's a warm-up which has a double function. There is some stretching but there is also movement with the ball. I tell them not to push the ball too far ahead. If you do that in a match and all of a sudden you are confronted with an opponent, you can no longer change direction with the ball. If the ball is stuck to your feet, in any given moment you can dummy, stop, turn back and so on. So it's also a warm-up in which they need to think about what they are

The U19s warming up with the ball

doing. They have to use the brain to keep the ball under control. It's not the usual running laps of the pitch, which is monotonous and gets on everyone's nerves in the end. Running with the ball in the hands also helps warm up the limbs of the upper body. Making sure that the ball doesn't drop requires balance and concentration. So: movement, coordination, technique."

The word which Corradini calls out most frequently to the players during the warm-up is "balance". As he explains: "If you don't have balance you can't do anything. You can't shoot, dribble, feint. When you have the ball at your feet, it's extremely important." But to what extent is balance trainable? "I couldn't tell you what percentage is innate and what is learned, but everything is trainable. As [former Milan and Roma coach] Nils Liedholm used to say, you can improve the way you strike the ball even when you're 40 – the important thing is application."

Technique – passing and shooting 15 minutes

The players execute a passing exercise in groups of three while in movement (see Exercise 1). Corradini demands that the ball is passed along the ground with the right weight, with the players always maintaining a perfect triangle. He repeats the word "distance" several times. "The hardest part is when you're moving backwards. It requires balance and you have to check the distances between you and your team-mates. In a match, you can't just think of your own position. You have to be aware of the position of your defensive or midfield partners. If you are too far ahead of them or too far behind, something is not working. Look at the ball, but also look at your team-mate as a reference point."

In the next exercise, three players form a vertical line, C-B-A, with about 4-5 meters between each. A passes to B, who returns it first time and then comes a few paces towards A; A passes the ball through the legs of B to C, who kills it and passes to B, who has now changed direction to face C; B returns it for C to pass it through B's legs to A. Each player takes a couple of minutes in the middle. Every player has to use first the right foot and then the left foot, as is the case in each of the warm-up and technical exercises.

"If they are going to improve they cannot do the exercises exclusively with their stronger foot. Once the basic lesson of the exercise has been absorbed, if you keep repeating it with the same foot it is no longer making demands and is no longer training them. When things become too automatic, they become boring. So you create problems for them to keep them concentrated."

The players then practice running towards the goal and shooting from around the edge of the box after playing a one-two with a team-mate (see Exercise 2). "This kind of exercise is useful shooting practice for the training ground but given the time and space the attacker has, it is the kind of situation almost never presents itself in a match. So once you've done it, you have to increase the level of difficulty."

The next exercise is more demanding. It involves killing a pass, moving beyond an imaginary defender and shooting from just inside the box (see Exercise 3). "The three poles represent three opponents. The ball arrives diagonally. You have to control the ball with a delicate enough touch to take you just beyond the last pole for a quick shot on goal. The poles are stationary but their presence still creates a psychological obstacle."

Initially, the exercise isn't working well because the first pass is frequently under hit. Corradini puts this down to the fact that this is the easiest part of the exercise so there is a temptation to ease off, not to fully engage the attention. Under-hitting the pass forces the attacker to slow or even to come back to collect the ball and kills the momentum of the move. He makes a point strongly to the players that the first pass must be weighted correctly. After that, the move starts to come together. The other mistake is that the striker sometimes carries the ball too far wide of the pole, which creates a difficult shooting angle, favoring the keeper. "You have to touch it lightly enough to take out that last defender and then – boom! – right away, you bang in the shot. It requires immediate coordination because in soccer you often don't have time to organize yourself."

Match 9v9 – 35 minutes
The match is played with normal rules on half the pitch. The play is very organized, with both teams displaying great tactical discipline. Corradini says that this is largely the fruit of the work that the technical staff have been doing in the past six months. "We have developed that playing style here. I have tried to communicate to them something important about soccer: much of the play

in a match is concentrated into the middle part of the pitch, where at any one time you might have 14 of the 22 players. If you have good wide players, as we have, you have to get the ball out to them quickly. One touch, two touch, then open up the play with a wide ball. The winger controls the ball and the full back then overlaps. We have worked a lot on developing play down the wings. We aren't a team which is strong in the air as we don't have tall strikers. So when the wide players get to the penalty area they have to look either for a hard, low cross or a cut-back to the edge of the area. We keep the ball on the ground because the opponents are frequently better than us in the air."

"I don't oblige them to play one- or two-touch during training matches. That would be unnatural, forcing them into a certain way of playing. I don't give orders like that because it's reductive. Instead, I say to the players: 'I'm giving you the freedom to play. When you can dribble in a situation that benefits the team, do it. But if I see you dribbling the ball inside our penalty area or when you have the option to play a short ball to keep possession, I'll tell you that you are not a very intelligent soccer player.' On the pitch, the player has to take responsibility for her own actions and take initiative."

"The great coaches I have worked with always told me that the best form of coaching is playing a match. Giovanni Trapattoni, Zdenek Zeman, Dino Zoff and many others have said this. You can practice 300 exercises but the game always throws up something else. The spaces are smaller, the opponents are real, you worry about conceding a goal, and motivation levels become crucial. That tension can make an easy thing become difficult. The Werder Bremen keeper made a mess of an easy catch against Juventus in the Champions League. It was an infantile mistake. Why? Because he had been the hero of the evening and thought that the game was won. He had a slight drop in his attention level and did something he didn't need to do. He went to ground in order to waste a bit of time. He lost the ball in the most banal way possible, Juve scored and his team was out."

Correcting errors

"If everything is done well and the errors are corrected, every single training session gives you a positive result. In every session, it's important that the coach corrects errors all the time because if he does not, the players will assimilate the wrong way of doing things. Part of correcting an error is explaining why something isn't working. Today, one of the girls hit about 10 shots on goal and didn't make a single error. A few months ago, she couldn't hit the target. I explained to her just one thing: if you don't position your standing leg the right way in relation to the movement of the ball, you will never be able to shoot properly. The ball will either run away from you or finish up under your body. This is about coordination. She applied herself and practiced the shooting exercises. First, we slowed the action right down to focus on the position of the supporting foot and then gradually practiced more quickly."

"Some of the girls, when heading the ball, get the take-off wrong. In order to protect themselves from being hitting in the face, they turn their body way from the flight of the ball. Like this, they will still make contact with the ball but will not be able to direct it. You have to coach the way to jump and attack the ball. We have done several specific training sessions on heading. But this is not really the kind of work that you can do too much of with a national team because you don't have the time. It should be done from the Soccer Schools onwards at club level."

La Manga Tournament, 11-18 March 2006
"This tournament will give me the exact situation of the strengths of my team. It's pretty much the same group of girls as we had in Israel with only about five or six new players who have emerged since then, as a result of our scouting work. We know virtually nothing about our opponents – Norway, France and Sweden. We know only that they are good teams from countries with a good base of women's soccer. It means that, as coach, I have to read the match and react. However, if there is really a big difference in the level of the teams, there is little you can change. All you can do in that case is to try to limit the degree of domination by the other team, but it's difficult."

"Our basic tactical formation is 4-4-2. The players find it easier to understand and this is not like a club team, where they can spend all week working out tactical formations. It takes less time to explain the 4-4-2 and it's flexible so that during the game, it can easily become 4-3-3 or 4-5-1, according to the situation."

Norway 3 - 0 Italy
"Just about everything went wrong in this match. We conceded a soft goal in the first couple of minutes. A big gap just opened up in our defense. I couldn't believe it. We also let in a goal from a handling mistake by the keeper. We made mistakes as a team and mistakes as individuals. Norway are a good team but not as good as we made them look. I was not angry but worried. I thought that if we went to the European Championship and played like this, we would make a show of ourselves. Afterwards, I said to the girls that I was worried but that I knew that they had it within them to play better. What I couldn't accept was that they seemed afraid of Norway. I said: 'I know that we don't have leagues to compare with theirs but they are just girls like you with two arms, two legs and a head.' I think that a large part of the problem was nerves, with it being the first game. I confirmed the same team for the second game."

Italy 2 - 0 France

"Against France, we got just about everything right. I stuck with the same team and the same 4-4-2 line up. The midfield was excellent. We were tight when they had the ball and when we attacked our two wide players gave them trouble every time. France are a strong team – they have three really top-class players – but our girls really drew on their character and their pride in this match and showed that they have the means to play soccer. I knew after this game that I was right to think that we have a good team and the final game gives me the opportunity to play all those players who haven't taken part in the first two games. I don't want to drag players all the way out here and not play them and also I need to know, if one of the regular first-team players is out, who is ready to step up. I'm not worried about the result against Sweden at all."

Italy 3 - 0 Sweden

"I completely changed the team, playing all those players who hadn't started in the first two games which meant using all of the younger players. This was an important game because it showed that we can play against even the best teams. Usually, Sweden put three or four past us but this time it was Italy that scored three. The key to the result was the mentality of the players after the France game, which unblocked them psychologically and helped get rid of that inferiority complex they have had when playing teams from northern Europe."

Overview

"La Manga is a fantastic tournament and I hope to bring the team back next year. Everything, from the state of the pitches to the food, was first class. From a soccer point of view, it was well worth coming as it allowed the players to test themselves against some of the strongest teams around. Now we can go to Slovakia in the knowledge that we don't have to be afraid of anyone. It doesn't mean we will necessarily win. In a game of soccer anything can happen and so you have to maintain the right balance between a belief in your abilities and humility. We will respect our opponents – Hungary, Holland and Slovakia – but we won't fear them."

So close to qualification

Italy went on to beat Slovakia 3-0 and Hungary 2-0. The team needed just one point in the final game against Holland to qualify for the European Championship but conceded the only goal of the game with seven minutes remaining and was eliminated.

Exercises

Exercise 1

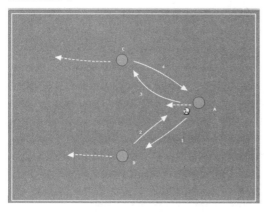

Organization: The players are divided into groups of three, forming a triangle. Player A, at the apex, passes to B, who kills it and passes it back to A. A then passes to C, who kills it and passes back to A. All the time the players are in movement. On the way out, A is moving forward, B and C backwards; on the way back it is the reverse.

Variation: Players repeat the drill using the left foot to pass.

Coaching: Well-weighted pass along the ground. Players always aware of the position of team-mates. Maintaining the right distance between team-mates. Good balance.

Exercise 2

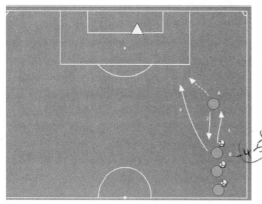

Organization: The players are lined up about 30 meters from goal towards the right of the pitch. Player A stands with back to goal about 10 meters ahead of the other players. Player B passes the ball to A, who returns it to B and then sets off on a run towards goal. B passes the ball ahead of A, who has to control it, take it forward a few paces and shoot from the edge of the area. B then moves to the starting point where A had been and repeats the move with player C.

Variation: Players repeat the drill using the left foot to shoot.

Coaching: Good, firm passing in the initial one-two. Positive run towards the box. Accurate pass which doesn't force the attacker to slow down or change direction. Good first touch to control the ball. Powerful strike with correct positioning of supporting foot. If the supporting foot doesn't leave the ground a little at the point of impact, the kicker is not using full power.

Exercise 3

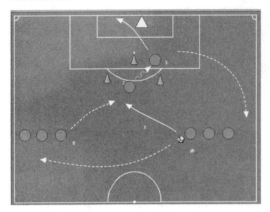

Organization: Three poles are placed in a triangle at the edge of the penalty box, with the apex nearest the goal. The players line up in two lines, at right angles to the edge of the penalty area, about five meters outside the area. Player A passes the ball diagonally to Player B who has started to run towards goal, heading into the space between the first two poles. B has to take one touch with the left foot to push the ball beyond the last pole and then shoot. A carries on running and joins the opposite line of players, B joins the other line.

Variation: Players repeat the drill using the right foot to control the ball and the left foot to shoot.

Coaching: Well-weighted pass which doesn't force the attacker to slow down or change direction. Good control with inside of foot, which pushes the ball just beyond the last pole. Powerful strike on goal with the right positioning of supporting foot. If the supporting foot doesn't leave the ground a little at the point of impact, the kicker is not using full power.

Part 3

Serie A and Serie B

Coaching in theory and practice

Chapter 1

JUVENTUS
Coaching the U20s, with Vincenzo Chiarenza

"No decent player is happy to lose a practice match"

Although 2006 will probably go down as a year to forget for Juventus Football Club, because of its role in the match-fixing scandal, Juventus remains one of the biggest names in world soccer. Founded in 1897, it is one of Italy's oldest professional clubs and by far the most successful. 'The Old Lady', as the club is affectionately known, has won the scudetto – the Italian league title – an incredible 27 times.

Vincenzo Chiarenza

At youth level too, the club is dominant. The U20 'Primavera' side won the prestigious Coppa Carnevale tournament in Viareggio, Tuscany, in 2003, 2004 and 2005 and reached the final in 2006. The team also won the national U20 league title in 2006, beating Fiorentina 2-0 in the final of the play-offs.

Since 2004, the coach has been Vincenzo Chiarenza, himself a product of Juve's youth system and an ex-professional player whose career spanned 15 years at the top level. Below, Chiarenza conducts a typical U20s training session, while Camillo De Nicola, head of youth soccer at Juventus [he has since left the club], explains the philosophy and organization of the youth set-up at the club.

De Nicola was in his second season in charge of Juve's youth system at the time of this interview, following many years in the role of director of sport or director

41

general at clubs like Cagliari and Ancona. His job description was very simple: "to produce boys who are fit to be professional soccer players." But, of course, it's never that simple. It's a long road from being a soccer-mad eight-year-old to stepping out in Serie A.

The early years: natural ability
Unlike the majority of professional clubs in Italy, Juve operates its own Soccer School, taking boys as young as eight years old. It has six teams of 'Pulcini', for boys between eight years and 10 years. Players under 14 cannot be signed from outside the region, but the club has an extensive network of observers working across the region to find the most promising youngsters.

"With today's technology, it's theoretically possible to get a good idea of how a child will develop physically, how tall he will be when he's 20 and so on," De Nicola says. "But frankly it's impossible to know if a boy of six or seven will make it as a professional. What our observers look for above all is natural technique. Only afterwards, do we look at the physical aspects."

The age of development: freedom to play
"In the first years, certainly until they reach the U17s, we focus on the technical development and not much on tactics. Our coaches let the youngsters express their natural ability as much as possible. We believe that a young player should go into a soccer pitch to show what he can do."

"We don't impose a club line on the way the players are coached. We leave each coach free to decide what's best. Each coach has the autonomy to plan the training in accordance with the characteristics of the players he has. At Juve and at the big clubs we let youngsters express themselves. If you go to some of the smaller clubs or into the provinces and into amateur soccer, it's very different. Even with the youngest players, the U8s, you get coaches who are just aping famous coaches. When they see one of their players dribbling, they start yelling 'if you don't pass the ball next time I'm taking you off.'"

"My idea is that the youngest players should play with no number on their shirts, with no fixed role; we should leave them free to go into the pitch and do what they can do, allow them to work out their own role without having a role imposed on them by the coach. Players of fantasy will emerge if kids are allowed to express themselves without being shouted at and told to pass the ball or play it first time. Soccer should be giving us the likes of Maradona, Ronaldinho and Ibrahimovic. But the young player with individual ability is suffocated by the fear of not being picked for the team and so soccer loses the player who can dribble. Soccer is fantasy and that should be made clear to all these pseudo-coaches out there who are running youth teams."

The final step: the elusive first-team place

"Once they get into the U20s, they start to do much more work specifically on tactics. This is the last step before full professionalism and when they make that step they will need to have a good understanding of tactics, positions and systems of play."

"The youth set-up at Juve is not constructed specifically to develop players for the first team but for professional soccer. Other clubs approach it differently. They don't have the same pressure that Juve does to get a result with the first team, to play regularly in the Champions League against the best teams in Europe. This means that we really can't throw in youngsters of 18 and 19 years of age. For many other clubs, given their financial situation, it is necessary to produce their own players."

"It's clear that at a club like Juventus there are not many boys who make it straight from the U20s to the first team but we produce hundreds of boys who go on to play at other clubs. Sometimes they are on loan or are owned jointly with another club, but we still look on their performance as being something we have produced. One day, maybe, they will come back to Juve and make it to the first team."

Preparing the U20s

The objectives of Vincenzo Chiarenza, coach of the U20s, are "to improve technique, individual tactics and team tactics and to develop the players psychologically so that they are ready to take the big step, so that they are ready to deal with first-team soccer on all levels." Tactically, he tries to stay close to the approach of the first team, but stresses that "this is my choice – nobody has imposed it upon me."

Chiarenza points out that in his three years in charge, around eight players from the U20s have played first-team soccer, although this has mostly been in lesser competitions like the Coppa Italia. He acknowledges the difficulty of establishing a regular first-team place direct from the U20s but says that this does not have a negative effect on the players' motivation. "The motivation levels are always extremely high. Of course, the objective of every player is to break into the first team but they know that if they don't there is still the possibility of going to another club in Serie A or Serie B."

Chiarenza's training session is divided into three phases. The first involves a combination of passing moves. The second is tactical work in a 9v9 game situation. The third is a 9v9 match with no restrictions. In between each phase there is some light work in the gym and some stretching. "It's Thursday today and we have match on Saturday, so we keep the physical demands relatively light. The work in the gym is not about building up muscle volume but rather just toning them up to help with speed and explosive strength."

Phase 1: combinations

Chiarenza divides 16 players into four groups of four, each group occupying, very roughly, a quarter of the pitch. They begin by knocking the ball around between the four players, with sharp accurate passes, mostly along the ground. Every few minutes, Chiarenza stops them and adds a new element to the exercise. This continues until the very simple initial passing sequence has mutated into a complex series of passes and movements.

At one stage, the exercise begins with the boys passing the ball around. Then, two players, A and B, have to 'take on' a third player, player C, executing a one-two to go around him. Player A, once has gone around C, kills the ball with one touch and with a second touch lays it back to the player C. As the ball is being laid back, player D starts a wide overlapping run. C hits a high ball first time which D has to head backwards. He has been followed by players A and B. A picks up the ball and plays a first-time one-two with B.

The whole first phase lasts around 40 minutes. "My primary objective in this phase is to improve the players' technical skills using situations which are likely to occur during a game." The exercise involves a range of passes – short balls and long balls, balls on the ground and high balls, quick one-twos – and different kinds of movement such as long sprints to overlap and quick bursts over short distances. Chiarenza is looking for several things: the timing of the run off the ball, good touch and control and accurate passing. He demands that the moves are carried out at high tempo. "We often start these exercises with a simple passing combination and then gradually build in layers of complexity. It's also work for the brain. The modern game is fast and physical and you have to think quickly."

Phase 2: timing

The 16 players are joined by two goalkeepers and divided into two teams of nine, playing with full-sized goals in one half of a full-sized pitch, for 30 minutes. Markers are placed about five meters in from the two touch lines to create two wide areas in which the player in possession of the ball cannot be challenged. The outfield players take up a 4-2-2 formation. The teams take it in turns to attack. The defending team in each move is passive: they close down the space and keep their shape but don't make tackles, so there is pressure on the man with the ball but not direct contact.

As before, Chiarenza begins with a simple move and then builds in layers of complexity. At first, the goalkeeper throws out the ball to the center-forward who controls it on his chest and lays it back to a midfield player. The midfield player knocks it wide to an overlapping full back who is attacking along one of the free zones along the touch line. He crosses for the attackers and the other midfield players to get a shot or header on goal.

Juve player crosses the ball into the box

Each move is practiced a couple of times by each team then modified, involving different target players, using combinations of passes between midfield players, and forwards making cross-over runs. The common denominator is that the move is rounded off with a ball played in from a wide player.

"What I'm really looking for in this activity is timing. It's about developing the timing of the pass and of the support movement off the ball, and the timing of the forwards in slipping their markers." Chiarenza wants every exercise to be conducted with the maximum intensity. He wants crisp accurate passing, a proper strike on goal at the end of every move and the right kind of movement from the forwards.

Phase 3: intensity

The final phase is a free 9v9 match in the same space with the same teams. The game lasts 15 minutes but is played with a high intensity. Although it's only a training match, everybody wants to win – something which is typical of the 'Juventus mentality'. As Chiarenza puts it, "I don't know any player of a decent level that is happy to lose a training-ground match." There are many shuddering challenges and Chiarenza says that this is necessary. "Tackles should never be made without the right level of concentration. It is a question of developing the right habits, the muscular fiber and the joints need to be accustomed to these kinds of challenge to be able to deal with them in a match."

"In the final match, what I want to see is that they have taken on board everything we have practiced in that day's training session, it should be a kind of summary of that day's work and the work of the earlier part of the week. But it's also true that the Italian player has a lot of creativity and fantasy so they also have the freedom to produce some individual creativity, especially in the last 16 or 20 meters of the attacking phase, where it makes the difference."

Exercises

Passing combinations: building layers of complexity

Part 1

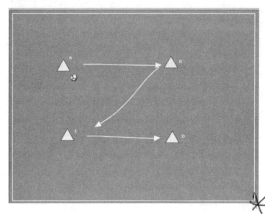

4-5 minutes. Four players have one ball and occupy an area which is approximately a quarter of a full-sized pitch. The players move around freely, exchanging passes and switching positions. The passes are firm and hit along the ground. At this stage the coach is looking mainly for quality in the passing technique. He gets particularly annoyed when passes are hit without sufficient strength. Stop. 1-2 minutes of stretching.

Part 2

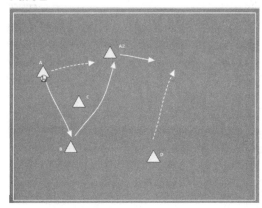

4-5 minutes. The four players continue to knock the ball around. At a certain point, players A and B 'take on' player C, and with a one-two passing movement they go around him. Player C is passive and doesn't try to win the ball. The players then continue to knock the ball around as earlier. In addition to the crisp accurate passing, the coach now wants the two players taking on player C to perform the one-two properly, with player A attacking player C at high speed before playing the ball to B. Stop. 1-2 minutes of stretching.

Part 3

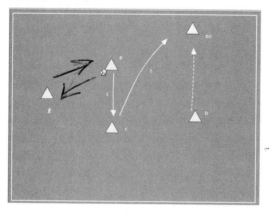

4-5 minutes. The four players knock the ball around and players A and B perform the one-two. Player B, on receiving the return pass, now has to kill it with one touch and play it back along the ground to player C. Player C then hits a long ball to player D who has already set off on an overlapping run. Player D brings down the ball and the four players carry on passing as before. In addition to the crisp passing and a good one-two, the coach now wants two further things: the correct timing of the overlapping run by player D (who takes his cue from the timing of the ball being laid back to C); and the accuracy of the long ball. Stop. 1-2 minutes of stretching.

Part 4

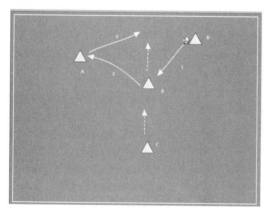

4-5 minutes. The move builds up as before, with passing along the ground, the one-two, the overlapping run, the long ball played to the wide player. Now, the wide player, player D, instead of just killing the ball and carrying on the passing movements, has to head the ball back to player B, who has moved up in support. Player B has to play a quick one-two with player A and then move away with the ball and begin again the original passing along the ground between the four. Player C, who has played the long ball, moves up in support. Now the coach wants to see all the earlier elements plus an accurate lay-off from player D, the right positioning of the support players and a rapidly executed one-two movement. Stop. 1-2 minutes of stretching.

Chapter 2

CHIEVO
Coaching the U20s, with Paolo Nicolato

"You have to maintain possession under pressure"

Chievo Verona have been the surprise package of Italian soccer in the last six years. The club, from a small suburb of the city of Verona, was promoted to Serie A for the first time in its history in 2001. Under coach Luigi Del Neri the team took the division by storm with exciting, attacking soccer based on a 4-4-2, "English-style" formation using fast wingers.

Paolo Nicolato

The club created its present youth-team structure around nine years ago and Maurizio Costanzi was appointed head of youth soccer. "Our objective has been to improve the players without being obsessed with results," he says. "In concentrating on improving the individual player we have arrived at a situation where we have also developed some strong teams. When we get to the stage in the season when they have a chance of winning something we will push for the result – but not at the cost of undermining all the work we've done."

Core values
Costanzi says that compared to youth coaching in France and Holland, which he has observed, Italian soccer still doesn't have the right balance between developing young players and getting results. "At the moment it's too focused on results. The politics of most big clubs is still to invest in the finished product rather than invest in the long-term job of developing players. A lot of this is linked to the high turnover in coaches which always creates the pressure to get short-term results. The clubs don't have the patience. We are a family club with a small fan base, so there is no pressure here."

He describes an episode as being typical of the Chievo approach. "In a tournament for the U11s, in the semi-final against Inter Milan, we scored a beautiful goal when one of their players was down injured. When our coach realized what had happened, he asked our boys to allow Inter to score a goal straight from the kick off. We lost the game but the team got an ovation from the crowd. This is our spirit. For us, sporting values are important."

No tactical fundamentalism

The U20 team adopts the same tactical approach as the first team, namely 4-4-2. Below that, there is no fixed tactical approach. As Costanzi puts it, "when kids go to school, they don't just learn one subject, they learn many. So we look at all possible formations: 4-4-2, 4-5-1, or whatever; defending zonally or man-marking, or a mixture."

Costanzi argues that "tactical fundamentalism" – the tendency for clubs to wed themselves to a particular tactical philosophy – is a thing of the past in Italy. "These days the objective is to create an intelligent soccer player who can adapt to all kinds of match situations, understanding the needs of the team. We develop a way of playing that is based on the characteristics of the players."

Two-year cycle

Chievo has a preferential relationship with 20 Soccer Schools in the region and works with about 70 in total. However, their "exclusive" arrangements are not always respected. "If a parent hears that one of the bigger clubs, like Juventus, is interested in their son, we can't do much. They don't always understand that by going to a club like Juventus rather than Chievo they won't necessarily have a better chance of making it as a professional."

The youth set-up has around 180 players in total, bringing in around 30 new players every season. For the newest recruits, the club tries to create a cycle of at least two years. "That's the minimum you need to assess them, so we tell their parents that we want them here for at least two years." Many kids stay all the way through the levels and some make it to the first team but, as Costanzi is quick to acknowledge, the hardest thing for a young player is to make the transition from the U20s to the first team. In the 2004-05 season, there were four or five players who moved between the U20s and the first team.

Under 20s

The U20s train every day for two hours and play a match on Saturday. The following session is a fairly typical late-season session. The head coach, Paolo Nicolato, is assisted by fitness coach Massimo Bucci and goalkeeping coach Carlo Romio.

Nicolato's session is structured around three match-play phases, after 15 minutes of warm-up activities and stretching exercises. The first phase is a possession activity with three variations, lasting around 40 minutes. The second phase is a small-sided game based on pressing the opposition, also lasting around 40 minutes. The third is an 8 v 10 match, based on defending when outnumbered, which lasts around 30 minutes.

Chievo passing warm-up

Nicolato points out that the boys are reaching the conclusive stage of the season and are experiencing a build-up of tension as key games arrive, so he tries not to overload them with information, especially of an analytical, tactical nature. "During the year, we do a lot of work on tactics, especially on Tuesday and Wednesday and on Monday we analyze the game they played on Saturday. They are a bit saturated with tactics now so I intervene rarely during training."

Each of the three activities is broken up into units of six or seven minutes with short breaks in between for stretching or for a drink of water. "Today is Thursday and they have a game on Saturday," Nicolato says, "so we don't want the physical demands to be too great."

Phase 1: possession

The players are divided into two teams of 10 playing across the pitch in the space between the goal area and the half-way line. They play a possession game with two variations. At first the players must carry the ball by hand, rugby-style, and pass it by hand, scoring a point when a player carries the ball over the opposition end line. If the player in possession is touched by an opponent while holding the ball, the possession passes to the other team. The first variation involves carrying the ball by hand but passing it by volleying it, as in Gaelic Football. The second variation involves two-touch passing, first with the right foot only and then with the left foot only.

"The tactical point of the session is maintaining team possession through movement off the ball but it is also a useful mental warm-up activity as it helps focus the attention," Nicolato explains.

So that the activity resembles a match situation as closely as possible, the players are organized into their normal positions in defense, midfield and attack (both teams in a 4-4-2 formation) and the off-side rule applies. Because the style of Chievo's first team is a flat back four which tries to push high up the field, all of the U20 training activities (which use full team line-ups) operate on these principles, so that when a player steps up from the U20s to the first team he is operating in exactly the same system.

Phase 2: pressing the opposition

The players are divided into two groups of 10. The first group goes off with the fitness coach, Bucci, for a series of exercises including stretching, posture work and explosive speed work. Each group spends 20 minutes with Nicolato and 20 minutes with Bucci.

Nicolato's group plays two-touch five-a-side in a small pitch. There are two cones at each end and three cones across the middle of the pitch. To score, a player must strike a cone at the other end of the pitch or one of those in the middle. The defending team adopts a loose 2-3 formation to be able to defend all five cones. The coach doesn't interrupt the play but uses brief instructions and key words to keep the players focused on the activity: "pressure", "closer", "keep it on the ground", "mark the cone", "show yourself".

As Nicolato explains, the primary tactical function of the activity is the pressurizing of the opponent in possession of the ball. "The fact that the attacking team can also score by hitting one of the cones in the middle of the pitch forces the defending team to stay compact and aggressive and to defend from the half-way line. The defenders have to stay as close as possible to the opponent who can turn quickly and hit one of the cones in the middle. This is a demanding exercise from a technical point of view because it is played at a high tempo. The player in possession has only two touches and is under pressure all the time. If a third touch is justifiable, I will let it go. But otherwise it gets blown up as a foul."

As in the first-phase activity, the movement off the ball of the attacking players is essential to providing options for the player in possession ("show yourself") and Nicolato looks for them to show a variety of movements to open up play, including one-twos and early long balls to the forwards.

Phase 3: defending when outnumbered

The players are split into two teams playing in one half of a full-sized pitch with the normal goals at one end and two small goals made up of cones at the half-way line. The defending team is made up of a goalkeeper, seven outfield players (divided into a back four and three midfield players) and two forwards who are stationed behind the small goals. The attacking team plays in a 4-4-2 formation and attacks at high pace. For the defending team to score, one of the midfielders must play a one-two with one of the target forwards before shooting into the small goals.

Unlike the previous two phases, here Nicolato does sometimes stop the game and step in to make a tactical point. "The match situation we are simulating is where an advanced midfield player loses the ball and the remaining midfield players have to defend the counter attack. There is just one central midfield player and two wide players and it is up to the wide players to compress the play when the ball comes into the middle of the pitch."

Coach Nicolato makes a point

"I was also asking the defending team to try to hold on to possession when coming out with the ball where they are outnumbered and there is no immediate outlet for the forward pass. But when the defenders are under real pressure I want them to hit the ball long and then push up quickly to compress the play."

During the exercise, players are switched between the two teams, maintaining their roles. "I always switch the players and mix them up. They are not divided into first team players and reserves, so every defender gets to play in the defensive back four, for example, not just those who will start the game on Saturday. That way, the less able players are mixed with the stronger players and they can learn from playing with them. On top of that, in this exercise there was no particular tactical requirement for the back four other than to defend the goal."

Exercises

Exercise 1

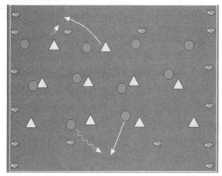

Organization: 20 players, in two teams of 10, play across the pitch in the area between the edge of the 18-yard area and the halfway line. Each team is organized according to the players' genuine playing positions, i.e. defense, midfield and attack. Normal offside rules apply. The players carry the ball by hand and must pass it by hand, to score a goal (or a "try", as in rugby) a player must carry the ball over the end line. If a player is touched by an opposing player while in possession, the ball passes to the other team.

Variations:

1) The players carry the ball by hand but must pass it by volleying it without letting the ball hit the ground. In order to score a goal, the ball must be played to a team-mate once the latter has moved into the space beyond the end line.

2) The ball is passed normally along the ground but players are only allowed two touches. To score a goal the ball must be passed to a team-mate once the latter has moved into the space beyond the end line. As a further variation, for two or three minutes, players are only allowed to use their left foot.

Coaching:

Rapid passing; timing of movement off the ball to lose a marker; beating the offside trap; pressing the player in possession.

Exercise 2

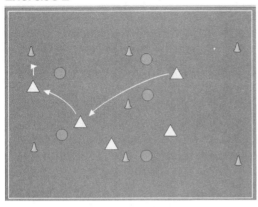

Organization: 10 players, in two teams of five, play on a small pitch, about 30m x 15m. Two cones are positioned at each end and three cones across the middle of the pitch. To score a goal the players must hit one of the cones at the other end of the pitch or one of the three cones in the middle. The players have two touches on the ball.

Coaching: Pressing the opposition; keeping the team compact at all times; making yourself available for a team-mate; quick, accurate passing along the ground.

Exercise 3

$$(4\text{-}4\text{-}2 \text{ vs } 4\text{-}3\text{-}2)$$

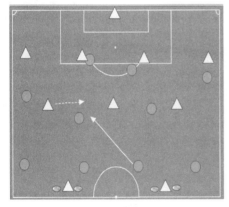

Organization: 20 players, divided into two teams, play in one half of a full-sized pitch, with normal goals at one end and two small goals made up of cones at the half-way line. The defending team is made up of a goalkeeper, seven outfield players (divided into a back four and three midfield players), plus two forwards who are stationed permanently behind two small goals. The attacking team plays in a 4-4-2 formation and attacks normally. For the defending team to score, one of the midfielders must play a one-two with one of the target forwards before shooting into the small goals. During the exercise players are switched between the two teams, maintaining their roles.

Coaching: The wide midfielders of the defending team must squeeze up into the middle of the pitch when the opposition is attacking through the middle; the defending team must try to keep possession when bringing the ball out if there is no obvious forward ball; when the defender with the ball is under pressure and can't find an outlet pass he must hit the ball long and the defense push up quickly.

56

Chapter 3

BRESCIA
Coaching U20s goalkeepers, with Claudio Rapacioli

"The keeper is always active, always reactive"

Brescia Calcio was founded in 1911 and is a good example of what is commonly known as a "yo-yo" club, having spent a good deal of its history bouncing up and down between Serie A and Serie B. The club followed an 11th-place finish in the 2003-04 season with relegation at the end of 2004-05 and was in Serie B at the time of this interview.

Claudio Rapacioli

Nevertheless, it has been home to some great players, including the legendary Roberto Baggio and Italy midfielder Andrea Pirlo, and is developing a good reputation for its youth set-up. One of the most tangible signs of this work is the coaching of young goalkeepers: Brescia is unique in Italian soccer in having three first-team goalkeepers who are products of its own youth system.

The man charged with converting the young goalkeepers from promising youth-team material into first-team regulars is Claudio Rapacioli, who has been at the club for five years and coaches the goalkeepers of the U20s. Below, Rapacioli puts four young keepers through their paces in a typical training session.

Footwork: think!

The session begins with 10 minutes of use of the ball with the feet. The goalkeeper has to control the ball with one touch and then play it out to one of three players – one situated to his right, one to his left and one straight ahead, each at a distance of about 20m. At first the ball is played as if under no pressure, but occasionally, to simulate a situation of pressure, the coach will shout, as the ball is arriving at the keeper's feet, "man to the left", or "man to the right". The keeper then must decide, quickly, which is the safest option for clearing the ball and maintaining possession. The way the ball is played to the keeper is then varied, forcing him to control it with different parts of the body such as the chest and the head.

Rapacioli wants a good first touch, for the keeper to control the ball with both feet (using the appropriate foot according to where the ball arrives), for the keeper to keep looking up as the play develops, and for the ball played out by the keeper to be accurate. Most of all, he demands speed of thought and the right choice of pass. Sometimes he stops the activity to discuss the choices that the keeper has made, other times he just shouts out key words like "think".

Footwork for a goalkeeper is an essential aspect

"A keeper these days needs to be good with his feet, not just in his positioning before a save but in his use of the ball. It very often happens that the ball comes through to the keeper along the ground or is played back to him by a team-mate. He needs to be able to control the ball under pressure and start the move going again by kicking the ball accurately."

Defending the goal, shot stopping

After the initial ball-work activity, the rest of the session is dedicated to defending the goal and shot stopping. Each exercise simulates a potential match situation. In the first exercise, five plastic markers are placed in a semi-circle at the edge of the six-yard area. Each one represents a player. The coach identifies one of the markers to the right hand side of the goal as the "opponent" carrying the ball, and he stands either centrally or to the left. At the coach's signal, the keeper has to move off his line towards the identified marker, as if closing down that "opponent", then switch his position to block a shot by Rapacioli, as if an opposing attacker had played a last-minute square pass for a team-mate to shoot.

In a second exercise, three three-step rope ladders are placed on the ground in front of the goal, at first in the form of a cross, later in parallel. In both cases, the keeper has to step in each square before making the save but in the first (cross-shaped) he has to change direction, while in the second, he is always facing forward. There follows a series of different exercises using two poles joined by a tape set at various heights, with the keepers either having to dive over or roll under the tape before either catching or punching the ball.

A final set of exercises uses poles and cones placed in front of the goal. The coach calls the number of a cone and the keeper must run past the poles, duck down to knock over the identified cone, and move quickly back to defend a shot on goal.

In each exercise, Rapacioli is looking for certain things: speed of thought and movement; the right body posture (a low, but not too low, center of gravity, the weight on the toes, head up to observe the shot); quick movement of the feet when changing position; good body strength in the save or punch; using the appropriate hand if a one-handed save is required; quick reactions to get the second ball if there is a rebound.

Reactivity exercise with poles and cones

"You will rarely see a goalkeeper making a save from a stationary position. He is always saving while in movement because he is reacting to a game in front of him with many, sometimes very subtle, changes of pace or position. So he constantly has to change from moving along a vertical axis to working along a horizontal axis and vice-versa."

"The main problems which young keepers face are those connected with the phase of anticipation of the save. There are two phases to making a save: anticipation and evaluation. Anticipation is made up of various factors: your starting position, your posture and body shape, and how you move. Many errors can be eliminated by working on these three components of performance."

Always reactive

Because Rapacioli uses a large number of different exercises during the session, each with three or four variations, the keepers don't work on a single activity for more than three or four minutes, so the level of concentration is high all the time. "You only need to change one small parameter within an exercise for it to become a radically different activity for the keeper. If I get them to practice exactly the same exercise seven times, the first time they will do it well, the second time they will do it quite well, but gradually their attention levels will drop and the seventh time they will do it badly. If they are used to maintaining a high level of attention for the full training session it will be easier for them to do so in a competitive match."

Even within a single variation, Rapacioli will still sometimes do something unexpected. He might hit four hard shots at a keeper, which they have to dive to save, but the fifth time play a short ball which they need to come off their line to claim. As he explains, "they have to be always reactive. In a match, they could see an opponent lining up to take a shot, so they get ready to dive to save it, but the ball might be deflected by a defender and change pace and direction, and they then have to do something completely different. The training should never be 100-per-cent predictable."

Always active
It is sometimes said that a keeper is called upon to help his team at only certain key moments of the game. "This is profoundly mistaken," says Rapacioli. "The keeper is active for the full 90 minutes but he has different jobs to do throughout that period. When his team is attacking, the keeper's job is to read the situation tactically. As a coach, I want my defense to be properly organized. If the defense becomes unbalanced and the goalkeeper doesn't see this and doesn't give the right call, I get angry with the keeper. When the opposition has the ball but is a long distance away, his job is to keep the defense organized and to begin to defend the space. If we tell keepers that their job is just to save shots and that they need to concentrate once the ball arrives in the final third, we run a big risk."

"A concentrated goalkeeper is one who anticipates and pre-empts actions by watching and by talking to his defense and guiding the team. A keeper who doesn't do this, and has a disorganized defense in front of him, might have to save 10 shots in a game. If he's good at reading the situation and at communicating, he will help the defense to pre-empt an attacking situation and as a consequence might have to save only five shots. So reading the play and communicating is equivalent to having saved five shots."

Analysis counts, video helps
"The ability of a coach lies in observing what kind of errors his goalkeepers are making and knowing how to correct them. Two different goalkeepers might, for example, be diving the wrong way to meet a shot, diving with their hands behind them – diving backwards, effectively – and not managing either to save the shot or to knock it away with adequate force. But the reasons for this could be different in each case."

60

"With one player it might be that he hasn't yet developed adequate upper body strength, with another it might be that he is placing a foot in the wrong position before the dive, starting off too far forward and then being forced to dive backwards. On the basis of analyzing these faults you can then plan the exercises which are necessary to correct them. For one player, it might just require more work in the gym. For another, it might involve, say, exercises with obstacles placed in front of him which prevent him from moving his feet in a certain way, which oblige him to move correctly and help eliminate the error from his game. Putting them through exercises without the right analysis is a waste of time."

"I use video a lot to help get these points across to them. It is an increasingly valuable tool for coaches, even for youth coaches. I video the keeper's performance in competitive matches and once a month someone comes in to video the whole training session. When I correct them or point out things to them in a normal training session the message still gets through. But when I talk it through with them and they can see themselves on video, it really hits home."

The modern goalkeeper

"The modern goalkeeper needs, above all else, to be alert tactically, to be able to read the situations of play. In the course of a game, a keeper may not be called upon many times to defend the goal by saving a direct shot. He will more frequently have to defend the space, interacting with the rest of the defense. The opponents will have a whole variety of ways of attacking the goal, from low through balls threaded through the middle to high crosses, so the keeper needs to understand how the move is building up, to anticipate what will happen next, so he is able to come out quickly to smother a low through-ball, to catch a high ball into the box, or whatever. For shot-stopping he needs good technique, co-ordination, reactivity and strength. The modern ball moves very quickly with strange trajectories, so you don't have time to think, you have to react very quickly."

Objectives

"Each season we start out with a series of different objectives. There are those of the club, which wants to have players coming through who are good enough to play for the first team. This is our primary objective. Then there are the technical objectives which I set, which are linked very much to the individual player. Having had time to get to know the players' strengths and weaknesses I know that there might be one keeper who needs to improve on coming out for crosses, one who needs to improve on diving to his right and so on, so I personalize the technical objectives as much as possible. There are also general objectives which apply across the board, such as developing the players physically, and tactical objectives such as learning how to read the game."

A typical week's training for Brescia's U20 goalkeepers

Monday: rest day or light training session
Tuesday: technical exercises for footwork,
               use of the ball with the feet when under pressure
               situational play, team tactics
               defending the zone rather than the goal
               physical work in the gym
Wednesday: defending the goal
               shot stopping
               speed and reactivity work
               gym work
Thursday: defending against high balls
               work in the gym
Friday: speed and reactivity
               tactical work with the defense and with the rest of the team
               based on different match-play situations
Saturday: match
Sunday: rest

Exercises

Exercise 1

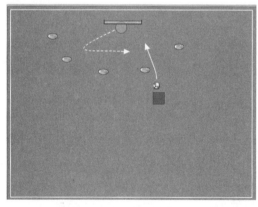

Organization: Five plastic markers are placed in a semi-circle around the edge of the six-yard box, the keeper starts on or near his line, the coach stands centrally just beyond the markers. The keeper comes off his line towards one of the wide-positioned markers, changes direction quickly, moves back into position to save a shot from the coach.

Variations: The coach changes his starting position and the keeper has to "close down" a different marker before moving to stop the shot – these two alter the axes through which the keeper has to change direction; shots arrive at different heights and different speeds.

Coaching: Rapid movement; light on the feet, putting weight on the toes; avoid a 'jumping' movement with is caused by putting weight on the heels; keep the head up; a strong dive to meet the ball rather than waiting for the ball to arrive at the body.

Exercise 2

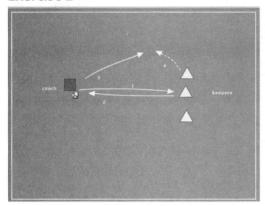

Organization: Two poles are placed about 8m apart, at one pole stands the coach with the ball, just in front of the other there are three goalkeepers, standing very close together. The poles are connected by a tape about 1m above the ground. The coach throws the ball at head height to the keeper in the middle four or five times in quick succession, then throws it to one side or other of the pole. According to where the coach throws the ball, one of the outside keepers dives to save the ball.

Variations: The ball is thrown or bounced at various heights, and various speeds. The activity is developed by placing the poles at 90 degrees to the goal line, about one third of the way across the goal, the keeper exchanges throws of the ball with the coach, then jumps over the tape and dives to save the coach's shot, other players are positioned around the goal to score on the rebound if the keeper doesn't hold the ball.

Coaching: Attack the ball, don't wait for the ball to attack you; move your feet quickly when changing position; keep the right body shape just before the dive with a low center of gravity but with the head up to see the shot coming; if you don't hold on to the shot first time get up quickly either to save a rebound shot or to smother it on the floor.

Exercise 3

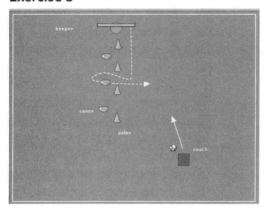

Organization: Four poles are placed at right angles to the goal line, half way across the goal. Interspersed with the poles, just to their right, are three cones. The coach stands to the right of the six-yard box and calls out a number between one and three. The keeper has to run vertically along the line of poles, move quickly to the right, knock over the cone whose number the coach has called out, switch position back to the left to stop a shot from the coach.

Variations:

The position of the poles and cones is reversed, so that the keeper always dives to his right rather than his left; the coach shoots from different angles, at different heights and speeds; other players wait to shoot on the rebound if the keeper spills the ball.

Coaching:

Attack the ball to get a strong contact, don't dive backwards; move the feet quickly by keeping most of the weight on the toes; keep a low center of gravity when preparing for the shot but head up; if you can't hold the ball first time, get up quickly to dive on the loose ball or to save the rebound.

Chapter 4

ATALANTA
Coaching the U17s, with Alessio Pala

"Technique is no longer an end in itself"

Atalanta Bergamasca Calcio, known simply as Atalanta, is from the city of Bergamo, near Milan. Inevitably, the club is overshadowed by its glamorous neighbors, AC Milan and Inter Milan. Atalanta cannot compete with the two Milan clubs in terms of buying top players like Adriano and Kaka but its youth set-up is a match for any Serie A club. It has produced many top players who have plied their trade in Serie A, such as Alessio Tacchinardi (with Juventus),

Alessio Pala

Tomas Locatelli (Bologna and Siena) and Domenico Morfeo (Parma). Indeed, for many observers of Italian soccer, Atalanta is a model of how a small or medium-sized professional club should be run. At the time of this interview the club was in Serie B but was promoted as champions at the end of the 2005-06 season.

Mino Favini, the head of the club's youth set-up, says that Atalanta is successful at youth level because the club doesn't just pay lip service to developing home-grown talent. It genuinely believes in its youth set-up, invests heavily in developing it and rewards youth players with promotion to the first team as soon as possible. The club has invested in a top-class training ground, with perfectly-manicured pitches and a state-of-the-art gym so even the youngest players – the 10-year-olds and 11-year-olds – are learning in a highly professional environment. The club has also deliberately chosen ex-professional players as coaches. They bring what Favini calls "the practical experience of the soccer pitch" and not just coaching theory.

One of these ex-pros is Alessio Pala, who at the time of this interview, was in his fifth season in charge of the U17s, after having worked up through the younger categories during the previous four years. The group trains three times a week for around two hours and plays a league match every Sunday. In the session below, Pala puts his 15-strong group through a two-hour session dedicated to attacking plays.

Attacking

The session begins with a 15-minute warm-up involving some 30-meter runs combined with some dynamic stretching. After this, Pala moves immediately into the first attacking situation. The players are divided into two groups, one operating from the center to the left of the goal and one from the center to the right. In each group there are two midfielders, one of whom plays as a winger, and two attackers, one of whom operates as a

central striker and the other as a second attacker, making a decoy run. The ball is moved quickly from the midfield to the attack and then wide for the winger to cross into the box where the two forwards and the other midfield player are arriving to attack the ball. Pala explains the maneuver very quickly to the boys and gets the activity moving at a high pace. As soon as the move is initiated by the midfielders positioned to the right of the pitch, the equivalent players on the left start begin their move, so that there are seamless waves of attacking moves.

Every four or five minutes, Pala quickly explains a variation required on the timing of the runs and the direction of movement. For example, the three players arriving in the box change the direction of their runs at the last moment so one attacks the front post, another the back post and the third the center of the area.

"This is a fast and demanding session, both physically and mentally. The boys understand quickly what I tell them and pick up the variations quickly. They have to be able to think quickly in a game situation and react to the changing nature of the game, putting into practice a variety of different plays according to the situation," Pala says.

Technique applied at speed

After 20 minutes, there is a short period of stretching followed by a short break for a breather and drink of water. Then the players take up their positions for the second attacking drill. As with the first drill, the basic pattern of the move involves an exchange of passes between midfielders and forwards, with the forward spinning off an imaginary marker and a wide player delivering a ball into the area for the players running in. It is followed by three or four variations, all explained and executed rapidly.

Pala says that speed of thought and speed of action are fundamental at this level: "This group of players has arrived with a very good technical base because they have worked their way through all of the other youth levels. So this year, we work on applied technique and on individual tactics plus we begin to work on concepts of team play – the relationship between the different units of the team: defense, midfield and attack."

"My objective for the season is to consolidate the technical lessons they learned in earlier years, then make the players apply that technique under the pressure of an opponent, increasing the speed at which they have to execute the technique. In previous seasons, they practiced the techniques and drills at low speed but now we speed things up a lot. The repetition of the skill in the most precise way possible with little space and little time on the ball is the key. Technique is no longer an end in itself."

After the second drill there is another short break followed by some sprints. Apart from a couple of short breaks the players have now been running hard, both in the drills and between the drills, for nearly an hour and have another hour to go. Pala says that most, but not all, of the boys at this level are ready for hard physical work. "In addition to the general conditioning work, you can work a lot on strength and speed, especially speed. You can't exaggerate the physical demands because there are still some players who are not as well developed as the others and you have to give them some space, to take things a bit easier with them."

Timing

In the third attacking situation, the players are in three groups, lined up vertically in the center of the pitch. The move develops as before, with a ball played into a target forward player who lays it off, one player going wide to cross and two players attacking the space in the area. As with the first two drills, the essence of the activity is timing. "The tactical key to all of these drills is the timing of the movement. What I'm looking for is the timing of the forward players in slipping their markers, the timing of the cross from the wide players, the timing of the runs into the box from supporting players and the timing of the shot on goal."

Pala says that in this kind of drill the players commit both tactical and technical errors. For today's session he is more interested in developing the tactical side and so spends very little time correcting technical errors such as a wayward cross or an inaccurate shot on goal. "The most common tactical error is to move too early or too late, especially on the taglio [cut-in] move, when the player has to switch direction suddenly to throw the marker and attack the space between the defenders. That's a very difficult skill to learn and takes time. It's something they will do a lot more of when they reach the U20s. The other errors are in the timing of the overlap, the cross and the shot."

Reference points

"When they go wrong, I try to correct them by giving them reference points. For example, the timing of the attacker slipping his marker depends on the timing of his team-mate receiving the ball. He has to make his move as his team-mate is getting the ball under control so I tell him to wait and watch what his team-mate is doing, make sure that he's got the ball under control. For the timing of the wide players making an overlapping run or support players making their move into the box, it's a question of watching the movement of the ball. For general guidance, I tell them not to get ahead of the ball. If they do so, they risk getting into an offside position or having an opponent anticipate the move and intercept the pass. For the timing of the strike on goal, I want it to be as quick as possible, even if that means sacrificing accuracy in the short term."

After another short burst of sprinting and dynamic stretching, the players start the fourth attacking situation. This is an 10v0, shadow-play team move in which the midfielders and two attackers (who start every move with their backs to goal) put into play in a more fluid team situation as many as possible of the moves they have been practicing earlier, finishing with a cross from wide and three or more players attacking the space in the box.

The players then round off the session with a 7v7 match in a 30m x 40m pitch, with Pala demanding a high level of intensity and concentration on the timing of runs.

Psychological strength

The whole session is fast, intense and demanding, but, Pala says, the boys need it and can handle it. "Psychologically they are already strong and mature. They have moved up a level this year and are now playing in a national league, regularly competing against teams like Juventus, Inter Milan, AC Milan and Cagliari, who all play at a high level. And now they are playing to win. It's still about growth, learning and development but it's also important to play to win and to get used to competing at a high level. There is greater pressure now – it's not over-the-top pressure, nothing's going to happen to them if they lose a game – but it's important that they feel that they can compete against anyone."

Exercises

Exercise 1

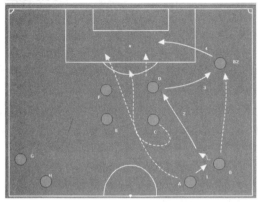

Organization: The players are divided between points A – H in one half of a full-sized pitch. The move begins just inside the half. There is no goalkeeper. A passes the ball to B and moves left towards the edge of the penalty area. B carries the ball towards C. C feints to moves towards him but then cuts back and also runs towards the center of the penalty area. Instead of passing to C, B passes the ball to D, who then plays it wide for B to cross, meanwhile D spins off and also moves towards the area. B crosses for one of the three players now attacking the space in the penalty box. One of the three shoots or heads on goal. Once players A-D have got the play under way, players E-H begin.

Variations: The attacking players switching positions as they arrive in the box. Every player plays on both the left and right, and so is forced to use both feet.

Coaching: The forward making the decoy run has to time his run to make sure that he doesn't arrive in the box too early and have to wait around for the ball to arrive, making him easy to pick up for the defender. The wide player must not get too far ahead of the ball. The players arriving in the box attack different spaces. The strike on goal must be as quick as possible.

Exercise 2

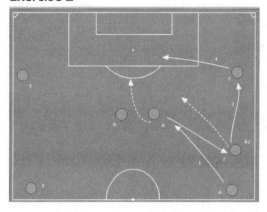

Organization: The players are divided into groups at points A to F in half of a full-sized pitch. The move begins just inside the half. A passes to B, who returns it into the path of A (at A2) and then spins off and heads towards the area. A passes the ball to C and also attacks the area. C either crosses or lays the ball back for one of the two players arriving in the area. A or B finishes the move with a shot or header on goal. As soon as the first player at point A has got the move under way, a player at point F begins.

Coaching: The players attacking the box must time their run to arrive at pace in the danger area as the ball is being delivered. The players attacking the box must attack different spaces. The strike on goal must be as quick as possible.

Exercise 3

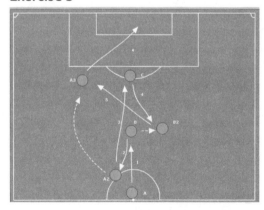

Organization: The players are divided into three groups at points A, B and C in half of a full-sized pitch. The move begins just inside the half.
A passes vertically to B and moves forward (to A2). B lays the ball back to A and moves a few meters to his left (B2). A passes to C and immediately goes to the left attacks the area. C knocks the ball back to B, who plays the ball forward diagonally into the path of A (at A3). A shoots on goal. Repeat with A attacking on the right hand side of the box.

Coaching: Player A must time his run so as not to get too far ahead of the build up play between C and B. B must time the pass to that A does not have to break stride. A must shoot first time.

Exercise 4

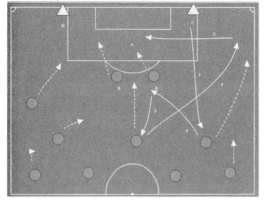

Organization: 10 players adopt a loose team formation with only the forwards at A and B, who have their backs to goal, having a fixed starting position. The play takes place in one half of a full-sized pitch.

One player, either C or D, stationed to the side of the goal on the goal line, kicks the ball long to one of the defenders or midfielders. This player initiates a move which brings into play one of the forwards, A or B. The ball is laid back by A or B to another midfield player and then knocked wide to another midfield player who has overlapped down the wing. The winger then crosses the ball into the center, where the two forwards, backed by one or more midfield players have attacked the space. The players should put into practice each of the variations they have tried in Exercises 1 to 3.

Coaching: The move will only flow if each player times his part of the play correctly.

Chapter 5

EMPOLI
Coaching the U17s, with Giovanni Vitali

"Everything we do here improves skills"

Tuscany is known to most people as a holiday destination not a hotbed of soccer but with Empoli FC now in Serie A the region has four top-flight clubs – more than any other Italian region. The club was in promoted in 2002, relegated in 2004 and bounced straight back up the following season.

Giovanni Vitali

Empoli was founded in 1920 and for most of its history the club operated in the lower leagues. The current president, Fabrizio Corsi, took over the club in 1991 and began investing to take Empoli up the ladder.

The investment has paid off both in the first team and in the youth set-up, on which Empoli spends around €2.2 million a season – more than most clubs of a similar size. The youth set-up has produced many players who went on to make their name with other clubs in Serie A, like Vincenzo Montella (Roma), Marco Marchionni (Parma and Juventus) and Mark Bresciano (Palermo). Empoli's U20s won the prestigious Coppa Carnevale in Viareggio in 2000 and came third in 2007.

"Empoli is a city of 40,000 inhabitants, so a club like ours cannot afford to buy big stars. We have to develop a good youth set-up. It's the only way," says Andrea Innocenti, who is responsible for player recruitment and technical development. "We have invested heavily for many years in the youth set-up and the results have been good, particularly in the last five or six years."

The financing of the youth set-up is guaranteed by the president and is not contingent upon whether the team plays in Serie A or Serie B. "I have been here six years – three in A and three in B – and I have noticed no difference in the way we work, no reduction in the budget. So we have the stability to work for the long term. Our fantastic sports complex was bought in the same week that we were relegated."

Of Empoli's first team squad in the 2006-07 season, 11 players are 'home-grown'. "The ultimate objective of our work is to produce players for the first team. Of the 22 players in the U20 squad in the Coppa Carnevale this year, 19 have been with us since the U15s, at least. Inter Milan, by way of comparison, had only four who had been there since the U15s. We are about continuity, about grooming our own players, and not about trying to bring in boys from all over the place just to get a result."

Soccer School launched

Empoli's youth set-up has 10 teams, three of which play in national professional leagues, three in professional regional leagues, and the other four in local leagues. Two years ago, Empoli launched its own Soccer School, which currently includes boys born in 2000, 1999, 1998, and 1997 – six-year-olds to 10-year-olds. The Soccer School is open to all children but when they reach 10 there is a selection procedure to see who will make it into the youth set-up proper.

In addition to the dedicated Soccer School coaches, many of the youth coaches from the older groups double up as coaches in the Soccer School, giving the school 12-13 coaches. This means that every group of players has four coaches working in each session, including two physical fitness coaches who work on co-ordination and motor skills and one former professional player who works purely on technique.

"The youth set-up is long-term project and we look for continuity. Until a certain age, the kids work almost exclusively on technique. Basic skills such as dribbling, and the use of the ball, from juggling to running with the ball, are the core. The key thing is touch, sensitivity to the ball. Once they get bigger there is also work on tactics and strength. I would say that 14 years old is the crossroads because they are going into the first national championship."

At the moment, only a small number of kids make it from the Soccer School to the club teams after selection and the club is hoping to increase the number in the future. "The important thing is that we make it clear to the parents at the outset what the route is for their kids," Innocenti says, "that we offer three years of Soccer School after which there is a selection. It's tough to say to a kid of nine or 10 that he can't enroll the following year, but it has to be done. Once selected, they are guaranteed three years of coaching at Empoli. When we make the selection, technique is the decisive factor, but physique is important to a certain extent and so is having some sense of position."

The club has 25 scouts in Tuscany, 25 in the rest of the country and four working abroad. With four Serie A clubs recruiting in the same region, there is competition to snap up the most talented boys but Innocenti says that Fiorentina is the only Tuscan club which poses a real threat to Empoli.

"Siena and Livorno [the other two Tuscan clubs] don't select boys this young and they don't have a youth set-up to compare with ours. Empoli offers a real chance to get into the first team and a first class coaching set-up. We are not worried about losing kids to the big clubs. The percentage that we lose like this is very small. We have established a reputation for youth soccer here."

Mental toughness
Until the U15s, the coaching work is largely technical but afterwards results become important. "The approach of the club is that the result is never more important than the development of the person. You can get players with ability who are idiots and we don't want that kind of player here; we prefer to have good players who also know how to behave. The rules are applied, even if that costs us a talented player."

Innocenti says that the mental aspect is fundamental in determining whether a player will make it or not. "Mental toughness. Desire. These aspects are the key and we work a lot on them. Can they be coached? Yes, but you have to start early. You have to lay down the rules. Here, kids of six already are given the rules, albeit in a 'soft' way, but they know exactly what they can and cannot do. That's formative. From day one, the coaches talk only to the kids about the coaching, never to the parents. Next year we will expand the rules to cover things like personal hygiene and diet, so that they start to become more professional in their approach."

"You have to find a balance between developing the player as an all-round player and producing a player for a specific role. By 12 a player should start to know how to perform a role, to play in a certain position, without ruling out the possibility that he could still change and develop into another role. By 14 or 15 you have to be good at your role, you should be close to being a player who knows how to do his job. With little kids, you also need to start working towards developing players in various roles because at that age everybody wants to be an attacker."

Coaching the U17s

Giovanni Vitali has been at Empoli for eight years and currently coaches the national U17 team, which, at the time of writing, was top of its league and heading for the play-offs to decide the national champion.

His big challenge this season, he says, was creating a cohesive team. "There were problems in the construction of team because the players had arrived came from three different groups. There were those born in 1991, who had been playing in a national U15 tournament. Those born in 1990, who had played in a regional U17 tournament, which is a useful formation but not as difficult technically as the national league, and then there were eight players who had already done one year in the U17 national league."

"To build the team, we had to identify a system of play that made best use of all the players. I was looking for growth from a tactical point of view – a bit more depth than last year – and also to improve technique in match situations. They all knew how to perform the skill in isolation but it was difficult for them to put into practice in a match."

"We have noticed, for example, that there has been a very significant improvement in the use of the weaker foot, in all players. There has also been an important growth in individual tactics. For example, the defenders have improved a lot on areas like positioning, tackling, intercepting, anticipation; this individual improvement has also improved the team unit."

"The team is good in build-up play and scores a lot of goals – an average of three per game this season – and at the moment we are first in the league, even though I would have to admit that the technical quality of the league this year is not exceptional."

"Having a top-quality sports center with artificial pitches has been a big help because we can plan the coaching and see it through, without being influenced by the weather conditions. Working on a perfect surface all the time also means that the players' touch improves. Until a couple of years ago, we might plan to work on something like running with the ball and have try to do it on a pitch that was in poor condition, which meant that you would end up having to change the work. Everything you do here improves technical skills."

Vitali does very little long-distance and middle-distance running for stamina – nearly all the running is done with a ball in some kind of soccer context – but does believe in work on strength in the gym.

"The warm-up is always based on technical work, regardless of what comes next. We do a lot of ball possession, in intense games, with cardio-frequency stats to check their heart rate, as this is the aerobic work which replaces running. For example, we do a lot of 5v5s with support players stationed around the pitch. There are lots of themed matches, with a tactical objective according to our monthly cycle. We don't get into tactical work on the basis of analyzing how our opponents play."

"This year, the match at the end of the session is nearly always played two-touch. This group has lots of very skilful players with a good touch and left to their own devices they would hang onto the ball too much. After a couple of months we realized that they weren't improving when playing with unlimited touches, so we imposed two-touch except for the last 7-8 minutes, when the fun aspect takes over."

In all Vitali's sessions there is work on match situations and individual duels: 1v1, 2v1, 2v2, 3v2, always with progressions built in. "This is the essence of soccer: 11v11 is basically a series of 1v1s in various parts of the pitch."

Session

On a cold March day, Vitali takes a session with 20 players in an artificial turf pitch of about 50m x 25m. There are three phases: warm-up, situational play and match play.

Phase one lasts 15 minutes. It is based on psycho-kinesthetic activities mixed with basic technique work. The players split into three groups, attackers, defenders, midfielders, with different colored bibs.

The U17s in a passing warm-up

Each group has two balls and the players begin by moving around, using the whole space, and trying to avoid concentrating in the same area.

Then there is a progression with a sequence of ways to pass and control the ball, within the color-coded groups. These include: one player takes a throw-in and another catches the ball with his hand; one player throws the ball with one arm and the other catches it; one player throws the ball, the other and controls it with his feet and moves away; the ball is passed with a volley on the inside of foot to a player who controls it and moves away; a volley with the instep, control and move; a half-volley and control.

Then the ball is played along the ground and the sequence continues. Two-touch pass and control; one player passes the other controls it before moving back and wide. Then two players of the same color create a one-two passing triangle around player of a different color. Then there is a sequence of long balls, over a distance of 25-30m, between players of same color.

"The psycho-kinesthetic element is the reaction to the colors," Vitali says. "This activity is improving their technical skills but always with an awareness of space and the movement of the others. The players of the same color should never occupy the same space. There are many variations you can do with the colors, like establishing an order in which the ball must be passed, and the direction of movement required after the pass. There is a didactic progression, with the activity getting harder each time. There is also a tactical dimension – the correct use of space (individual tactics) which is then applied in a match. The forward, for example, who must look to lose his marker by moving horizontally, the wide player who gives the ball and then goes on an overlapping run."

"Sometimes, as a warm-up, I get all the players in the center of the pitch and assign each corner of the pitch a different color. When I call the color they have to run there and the last one there pays a penalty. Sometimes when they are running towards one corner, I call another color and they have to change direction. Then they do all this with the ball. So they have to combine speed of reaction with technical skill. Every warm-up must have a playful aspect. It has to get the blood moving without being too intense but it must also improve them."

Phase two lasts 25 minutes and is carried out with half the group, while the other half works out in the gym. It is a situational exercise: 3v2 with a keeper, progressing to 2v2 with a keeper. The offside rule applies throughout.

The 3v2 starts with a long ball out from a player stationed behind the goal. The central forward player knocks the ball down to one of the wide players then overlaps. Then there is a series of passes and overlaps with one player attacking the central area and the other two moving wide. The attackers in groups of 3, defenders in pairs, rotate, so that one is active and the other is resting. Vitali calls for pace and rhythm and is always looking at the quality of the pass from the forwards, but this is an exercise for attack and defense.

"Although it may have looked like I was focusing a lot on the attackers, I was also working closely with the defenders. We have eight defenders here who still have a bit to learn tactically. I was looking closely at the posture of the defenders, how they turned, making sure that they weren't covering the same ground, knowing when to attack the ball, knowing when to close up the space.
78

We have two central defenders who are very tall, and if they are unprotected they can have problems with fast skilful players running at them."

From the 3v2, one attacker is removed. "The 2v2 is a progression and helps to verify if the attackers have learned the lesson of the 3v2, which is to always take on the defender in a 1v1 and use the overlapping player only when necessary." The group which has been in the gym now comes in and Vitali repeats the activity with them.

Phase three is a match-play phase lasting around 30 minutes. It is a 10v10 match, which is played two-touch except for last 7-8 minutes. The offside rule applies.

"The final match is very intense, and given the number of players in such a small pitch there is very little time or space on the ball, which helps to significantly improve the skill level and touch on the ball. There's constant pressure, speed and skill."

"I always like to play the match with 20 players, two complete teams. Everything is geared to the formation of the team, which is 4-2-3-1. So we train with four defensive players against six attacking players."

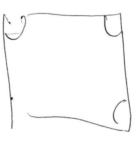

Exercises

Exercise 1

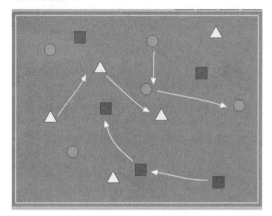

Organization: The players are divided into three groups according to their usual team role, defenders, midfielders and attackers. Each group has a different colored bib. The players have to move around the pitch, finding space.

There then follows a sequence of passes, in which one player in the group passes to another, beginning with passing and controlling by hand to passing and controlling with different surfaces of the foot. The technical demands of the pass and control increase as the session goes along.

Coaching: Occupy all the space on the pitch, without bunching in color groups. Awareness of how to move into space in relation to both own team mates and opponents. Accuracy of passing. Speed of thought, rapidity of the execution of the passing and controlling skills.

Exercise 2

3 v 2 / ½ pitch

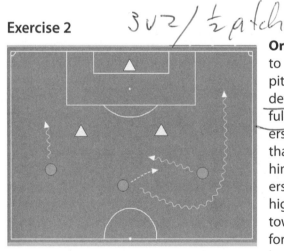

Organization: One group goes to the gym, the other stays on the pitch. Three attackers take on two defenders plus a keeper using the full length of the pitch. The players who are not involved in that moment are stationed behind the goal. One of these players begins the move with a long, high ball played down the field towards the central of the three forwards. He has to control it and lay it off quickly to one of the wide players. The player receiving

80

the ball immediately attacks one of the two defenders and tries to get past him to get a shot on goal. The offside rule applies. The two wide players try to offer different support options to the player with the ball.

Coaching:

Attackers: Good first touch; speed of passing and movement off the ball; crisp accurate passing; keeping onside in the overlapping runs; attacking the defender at pace, only using the overlapping player if necessary; powerful, accurate shot on goal.

Defenders: Good body posture for starting position to allow the greatest flexibility of movement and quickest reaction times; closing down the space quickly; not both attacking the same player or space; awareness of the movement of wide players; good strong challenge or interception if possible, otherwise hold up the forward without committing to the tackle.

Attackers Eric, Yunky Soubin, Henth,
Saam, [Julee?] [Ryel] [Thomas] [[Steven]

Mids [Steven] Spencer, Phillige, [Jesse] Kial
Josh, Jackson.

Backs Jim, Thomas, [Kial], [Phillige] [Jackson]
[Jese]

Chapter 6

RAVENNA
Fitness coaching for the U17s,
with Massimo Catalfamo

"Fitness training now becomes fundamental"

Ravenna Calcio has its origins in a multi-sport club called Unione Sportiva Ravennate, which was founded in 1875. After a series of mergers with other sports clubs in the late nineteenth and early twentieth century, the club began to take on something of its modern identity in 1928 with the foundation of AC Ravenna.

Massimo Catalfamo

The club has spent most of its life playing in the third division, Serie C, but in 1995-96 made the great leap into Serie B. The club collapsed in 2001 and had to begin life again, as Ravenna Calcio, in a regional league. Within six years, the team had climbed back into Serie B, where it remains, battling to avoid relegation once again.

At the beginning of the 2007-08 season, the club appointed former professional player Oscar Tacchi as sporting director, with responsibility for the youth set-up. Tacchi was recruited from local club Faenza.

"I worked for 10 years at Faenza, which is a small club. We had four years in Serie C2 with a bunch of local lads," Tacchi said. "Ravenna is a bigger club and has to build a youth set-up which is going to pay dividends in four to five years time. There's no point just looking for boys of 15 or 16, we have to start looking at boys of eight, nine and 10."

"We don't have our own Soccer School but we work closely with a number of clubs. A lot of small local clubs rely on income from their Soccer Schools and if we set one up here we would kill them. Clearly if there is a talented young kid out there sooner or later he is going to come to Ravenna. However, in this area we have to compete for the best young players with Cesena who have a great youth tradition which has been going for years. They have continuity on their side and we will have to work hard to catch up with them but we are not frightened of hard work."

Limitations of the Italian system
"I like the English system with a team manager, because he gets to understand the real situation of the club, what money there is to spend and so on. In England, a manager follows all aspects of the club and that includes keeping a close eye on the development of the youth set-up. Here in Italy the coach just coaches the team. Then you have the sporting director and a director general."

"In Italy it's rare that you have a great relationship between the first team coach and the coaches of the youth set-up. The first team coach is focused on obtaining immediate results, because this is what the fans demand, not on the long-term development of young players. The ideal situation is where the youth team coaches and the first team coach are part of a common program. Look at Ajax: they work with the youngest players in a way that follows right through to the first team. They learn the same systems of play, so that when they get to the first team they have nothing to learn. In Italy, the coach at each level uses whatever methodology he deems fit."

"I'm not saying that a coach should not have some autonomy but it should be within limits. Professional coaches, even in the youth set-up, have to remember that they are company men. This is a business not just a sporting club. There are big investments and as in any business you have to set your-self objectives and map out a way to achieve them. We give them a course, a direction, and the coaches have to adapt to this even though it's obvious that they must have some freedom in the management of their squad. A club, and its youth set-up, must have a philosophy and a soul."

Daily routine
"I work at my desk every morning on organization and spend the afternoon going around the various pitches to speak to the coaches and see if they have any problems. We talk about what has to be done next week. We program the work coming up in a way that wasn't really done before my arrival. Unfortu-nately, we have some obsolete facilities and some poor pitches but we are get-ting there on the organizational front. We are getting the sanitary and logistics side in order. The president wants to build a new sports center which would make our work much more efficient. We need four or five high quality pitches with one or two all-weather surfaces."

"All our plans depend on Ravenna staying in Serie B. The economy of any club is dependent on the results of the first team and if a club has to cut back, the first area it cuts is the youth set-up. If we go down to the third division it will knock the youth sector back a couple of years."

"I would like to employ a psychologist. When you have so many youngsters you can't know what's going on with every one of them, who has problems at school, who has problems at home and so on. We don't have a dedicated skills coach either. It's not easy to find someone who knows how to teach skills but we are looking for one. My plans are quite grand but it is something which takes time. We're growing slowly but we'll get there. For the moment, our top priority is to improve technique with good coaching. You also need good fitness coaches who understand how to develop players physically without doing them any damage."

Fitness coaching: working in stages

Massimo Catalfamo was hired as fitness coach at the outset of the 2006-07 season and at present works with the U20s and the U17s. "These are two age groups where the level of fitness work increases dramatically compared to what came before, up to the U15s. It is now that fitness training, in addition to the technical and tactical work of the first team coach, becomes fundamental," he says.

"When you're developing a young soccer player you have to work in stages. These must be related to the chronological age but, more importantly, to the biological age of the players. Usually, the physical development of a young-ster doesn't coincide with his chronological age. With small kids, a group will always be heterogeneous – some will be very well developed physically, others a bit behind, either for purely physical reasons or because their motor experi-ences are more limited. Often they will have started later, and will have less experience of sporting activity. You have to take this into account when plan-ning your work with 6-12 year olds. Everyone has to play, not just as a prin-ciple of fair play, but to give everyone as much motor experience as possible."

"A scrupulous didactic progression is required from 6-8s, to 9-10s to 11-12s. For example, with the smallest kids in the Soccer School, all activities have to be presented in the form of fun and games, a ludic activity. These games have to be geared towards developing the basic motor skills: running, throwing, catching, jumping – all the basic movements which will operate as a support for the later activities and stages. If a young kid doesn't know how to run in various ways – forwards, backwards, sideways – he will later struggle to do other things. You also have to train their coordinative abilities. These must be worked on right through from eight to 14 years, especially around 12 years."

Coordination and technique in the early years

"When working with younger players, I like to marry coordination work with technical work. For example, within the same exercise I use a circuit based on coordination skills, before passing directly on to a 2v1 situation, so the player concentrates on the coordination exercise before he gets to the ball. The skills of the game – controlling, running with the ball, passing – are all interrelated in a match situation: the ball arrives, you control it and then move with it before passing it. It is a chain of actions. If you do a situational activity where the player is just standing around waiting for the ball to arrive, it is less like a real game situation."

"Work on coordinative skills has to be done right through the youth teams, especially with the U15s when there is a growth spurt which can unbalance the youngster. Up to this point, the player has absorbed and consolidated certain abilities but increasing in height, for example, can dismantle everything. The youngster once again has to adapt to the changes in his body. So he has to revise and improve these skills. This carries on to the U17s and U20s, where you bring in work on agility, varying as much as possible the situations."

"If youngsters always do the same thing, they will lose their enthusiasm for coming to training. You need imagination, especially with the little ones. You have to vary the input, the games and activities as much as possible. If a game lasts 18 minutes, every 4-5 minutes you need to vary the game, provide a new input by adding some fun new rules. This is less important with older players, but variation can still help motivate players at higher levels."

The U17s: a typical week of fitness work

The U17s play in a national league with a match every Sunday. The athletic preparation is spread out during the week as follows:

Monday   Rest

Tuesday   Intermittent aerobic work: gradual build-up of speed to a high intensity over a distance of 75-85m; recovery periods, either active or passive, e.g. 15 seconds slow, 15 seconds fast, 30 seconds slow, 30 fast. Blocks of two series of 8-9 repetitions, lasting 6-8 minutes in total. Then 5 minutes with the ball, as recovery.

Wednesday   Strength work (see below)

Thursday   A friendly match. "After strength work, I avoid a competitive match, as the risk of injury is higher because the neuromuscular proprioception [the perception of information from signals from within the body] is altered."

Friday   Work on rapidity, reactivity and speed.

Sunday   Match

U17s fitness session, Wednesday 17 January 2008

Today's fitness work, with 14 players, is based on strength.

3.15   Warm up: light jog, a variety of movements for upper and lower limbs

3.25   Circuit 1: players split into three groups, two work with different rope ladders laid out on the ground, the third with wooden balancing blocks and plastic discs. Each circuit requires a different length of stride. Each group performs each stage six times then switches to next.

3.40   Circuit 2 and Circuit 3: two groups split between two circuits. The group performs the circuit four times then switches to the other.

3.55   Elastic rope exercises

4.00   Transformation on rope ladders

4.05   Match with first team coach, Cristian Minguzzi

4.55   Cool down

5.00   Ends

The methodology

The warm up
"You have to plan the warm-up for a session based on strength work in a very detailed manner. It lasts slightly longer than other warm-ups. The muscle has to be ready to deal with a greater workload. We do 15-20 minutes without the ball. It is a combination of a slow jog with work for the mobility of the joints, dynamic stretching and then some static stretching. Between the stretches we work on gait and stride, with a high skip or kicking up the heels behind, using double-impulse jumps and so on."

Circuit 1

Before moving onto strength exercises, there are some preparatory exercises, which help create the base for the necessary adaptation to the strength work. "I link proprioceptive exercises (on the wooden balance) with progressions (e.g. 4 x 60-70m at 70 per cent of maximum output), or progressions in limited spaces, such as with the ladders on the ground, as we did today. The proprioceptive exercises prepare the muscles for what they

Ravenna players do some ladder work

will do later on. With exercises on progressive speed, where the stride length increases, the ideal number of repetitions is from four to six. I want maximum intensity in the exercise, with an active recovery such as a slower return." Then there is a pause of 30 seconds before the next run. This gives an overall ratio of 1:10 between exercise and recovery time. Between one station and another there is a further two-minute rest. On a very cold day, it would be less.

In the recovery periods there are sometimes stretches, mostly for the flexor muscles. "There is always an imbalance between strong quadriceps, which are called into action a lot during soccer, and the flexor, which is a delicate muscle. They are the muscles which are first into action and therefore first to experience trauma. I pay almost maniacal attention to looking after the flexor muscles in the legs. The stretching is also related to the type of stretching done earlier, in the warm-up. When you do strength work, the burden on the muscle has the effect of shortening the muscle by three to four per cent. So you need to give the muscle back its elasticity."

Circuit 2

"I used the Cometti method, based on a combination of types of muscle contraction. During a match, a muscle works in three ways: in an isometric manner (the same muscle length), a concentric manner (shortening and lengthening) and eccentric manner (lengthening). In this circuit I combine isometric, concentric and plyometric exercises."

Stage 1: player seated with back against the post with legs bent at 90 degrees, for 15 seconds (isometric).
Stage 2: jumps on the benches with knee bends (concentric).
Stage 3: jump the hurdles and sprint (plyometric).

88

"With the U17s I don't go beyond this. With the U20s, or adults, you can also do work based on eccentric muscle activity. When a muscle expands, it expands eccentrically. This is the point at which most injuries take place. There are groups of muscles which are simultaneously linked to two joints and so are working in different ways in the same time. These muscles tend to suffer traumas and lesions. The flexor is one of these. Another is the rectus femoris muscle."

Circuit 2 - Stage 3

"The first stage works the quadriceps. Then we do the jumps on the benches – three on left side, three on right side – followed by jumps with legs together over the hurdles. The final part – the high skip and the 3-meter sprint is the 'transformation'. The transformation in any activity is the part which converts the strength acquired by the exercise into speed, which helps them to achieve greater explosive force."

Circuit 3

"This one is for the calves. We start with an isometric position of the calves, with the player stretching on his toes, while held down by a team mate applying pressure on the shoulders. Then there are 5-6 dynamic, explosive movements of the calves while balanced on the edge of the wooden block, held by a team mate or coach. This is followed by the jumps over low hurdles, and then the transformation: a double-impulse jump followed by 3-4 meters of sprint."

Elastic rope exercises

The players are divided into pairs, each pair with an elastic rope. Here there are four types of movement:

-       a high skip against the resistance of the elastic for 10 seconds. One working, one pulling, then swap.
-       see-saw movements in different directions, towards the right, towards the left, followed by the transformation (the same movements without the elastic)
-       a run with kicking movements against the resistance of the elastic for 10 seconds
-       see-saw movement, forward and backwards

Transformation

After this final bit of strength work, there is a final period of transformation, based on agility and speed, on the rope ladders. This requires rapid footwork and rapid changes of direction.

Cool down

"In the strength sessions you have to finish off with a few minutes of posture work to relieve the pressure on the spinal column. We have 6-7 basic exercises." These include:

- getting down on all fours and arcing the back upwards;
- on all fours and lowering the back, flattening the lumbar area;
- sitting with the buttocks on the heels, trunk straight, arms out stretched;
- the back flat on the ground, knees brought up to the chest;
- back on the ground, one leg stretched out, the other brought up to the chest, then switch legs;
- the 'Greek position', crossed legs, arms open at 180 degrees;
- leaning on the fence and sitting on their heels (this allows for a lengthening of the spinal column).

Chapter 7

FIORENTINA
Coaching the U15s, with Stefano Carobbi

"Professional soccer makes intense technical demands"

From 1926, when Fiorentina was founded, through to the turn of the century, the club from Florence was one of the big names in Italian soccer, one of the so-called "seven sisters" – those clubs who every year had a reasonable chance of competing for the title. The 'Viola' – the nickname comes from the unmistakable purple strip – won the league in 1956 and 1969, won the Italian cup six times and also won the Uefa Cup Winners' Cup.

In 2002 the club went bust and was kicked out of the league, having to start again from Serie C2 – the fourth division. Fiorentina was bought by the Della Valle family whose investments and shrewd choice of personnel had helped bring the club back up to Serie A by 2004. In the 2007-08 season the club is keeping pace with champions Inter Milan at the top of the table and powering through its Uefa Cup group.

In 2005, owners Diego and Andrea Della Valle made two inspired choices: former Parma coach, Cesare Prandelli, was appointed to coach the first team and Pantaleo Corvino was recruited from Lecce to be sporting director.

Corvino lands in Florence
Pantaleo Corvino had made a name for himself by producing incredible results in the youth set-up at the small southern club, Lecce, and by discovering a whole string of young players who have gone on to be stars in Italian soccer. These include: Fabrizio Miccoli, Christian Ledesma, Mirko Vucinic and Javier Ernesto Chevanton.

After seven years at Lecce, from 1998 to 2005, Corvino took up the post at Fiorentina. "My job at Fiorentina is to bring players through the youth system who will be ready for the first team and who will have value at national and international level. This was my job at Lecce, where we won seven national league titles, and at Casarano (in Serie C1 and B) where we won the U20s championship and where I brought through players like Paolo Orlandoni, who's now with Inter."

Corvino outlined his duties as sporting director at Fiorentina: "As the person responsible for the technical side at the club, I am called upon to marry the technical requirements of the first team with the technical development of the youth system. The technical resources of a team cannot be only measured in terms of what you go out and buy but by what you produce internally, within the club, starting from the youth teams. This is what I have done wherever I have worked, for over 30 years."

Philosophy: professional soccer demands results
"There are two types of soccer: soccer as fun, where you just play to enjoy yourself, and professional soccer, where there are huge economic interests. At this level, soccer is not primarily a ludic activity. Professional soccer makes intense technical demands and requires results. I am in one of Italy's biggest clubs and have to ensure that the sporting results are linked to economic results. To achieve these results you need time and high quality work."

"You have to make a distinction between the work with the first team and the work of the youth set-up. In the youth set-up the starting point is to create a structure in which you have the right man in the right job, to appoint a coordinator for very area: health, logistics, organization, technical work and recruitment. Then within each area you have sub-areas with the right people who follow the club line. In every area I tried to save the best of who was there already, because you don't always need to throw things away to make improvements, but I also put in lots of new people, especially in areas like recruitment and youth coaching."

"With the first team, you have to trust the coach to take care of the technical side. At club level we have owners – the Della Valle family – who are industrialists, bringing a managerial mentality into soccer. One of the things which characterizes this club is the attempt to marry sporting success with an ethical approach. This is part of our philosophy and is due to the Della Valle family."

Developing young players
To explain the secret of discovering talented young players, Corvino makes a distinction in Italian. It's about the difference, he says, between vedere (to see) and intravedere, which the dictionary gives as "catching a glimpse of". Corvino is talking about something halfway between observation and intuition. "Almost anybody can see a decent player but understanding that player's poten-

tial is the work of a specialist. What happens on the pitch will ultimately be the test of whether you can make that call."

Once the basic talent and potential has been identified, the rest is down to the quality of the work done by and with the player. "You could talk about what it takes from the player to make it to the top level but the most important thing is having good instructors. The first thing is not to ruin a young player of potential, then to have people who can add something to the player through the quality of their work."

At the moment, there are no players from Fiorentina's youth set-up in the first team squad. This may seem at odds with Corvino's philosophy, but as he explains, it is still too early in the cycle to see the fruits of the revamped youth system's work: "This club has just come through a very turbulent period, which had a profound effect on the youth set-up. When you have to start again from the fourth division, it's not easy to convince a talented young player to come to Fiorentina, even though it's still a big name. The process of overhauling the youth system only really began just over two years ago, so we are still putting down the roots, the foundations of what we hope will be a beautiful building. You need a cycle of at least five years to put things in place, after which everything runs automatically."

Recruitment and care

Fiorentina's youth set-up has around 180 players, beginning with the "Pulcini" category of children born either in 1998 (U10s) or 1997 (U11s) but the club doesn't have its own Soccer School. There are three teams of U10s and three of U11s, all of whom have to pass a selection procedure to join the club. The key aspect in the selection is technical skill. But not all the boys will make it beyond the first level. "We try to make a quick decision about which of these boys ought to carry on through the other age groups. For me, it's vital to let them know early whether it is worth them continuing to make a sacrifice or not. It's something I feel as a big responsibility having to say to a boy of 13 or 14, 'you should push yourself hard to make it' or 'soccer is not for you, you should leave it'. I have to have answers for their families as soon as possible."

The club runs a project called "Promessa Viola" for the 26 boys who have joined the club from outside the Tuscany region and therefore live in special accommodation provided by the club. "This is an innovative project which even Uefa has expressed interest in. We follow these boys step by step, monitoring the development of their character and ethical behavior. We have five tutors, who have a very important role in looking after the boys, helping them to solve their problems and reassure the parents that their children are being properly looked after."

"The Della Valle family wants to create the best possible situation for the children and to make sure that there is a proper substitute for their normal family life." For all the boys of the youth set-up there are also members of staff who maintain continuous contact with school and with the families. "When you take boys as young as nine, you have to make sure they are looked after," Corvino says.

Common objectives, different approaches

Corvino says that while all levels of the club share common objectives, each coach has autonomy in running his section. "You have to treat coaches the same way you treat players. Not every player is the same – each one has his own ideas, his own creativity. We get together every week, with the coaches and fitness coaches from every level and we exchange ideas but also try to ensure that we are faithful to the club's objectives. In the youth categories the main job is to develop the players technically, rather than tactically. The tactics – things like team formation – are always dictated by the players you have available, so you can't have a common tactical approach at all levels. It has to be based on the characteristics of the individuals."

In just over two years, Fiorentina has had good results at many levels, losing the national title at U17 and U20 levels only in the final. "Results at youth level are important in as far as they can provide a guide to whether you're going in the right direction. Good results don't come by chance or by themselves, they are the product of the right kind of work. But they are not the absolute priority. The real result for us will be when we bring a player through to the first team, which hopefully will happen in two to three years."

Coaching the U15s: Stefano Carobbi

One of Corvino's "right men in the right job" is Stefano Carobbi, coach of the "Giovanissimi" level, equivalent to the U15s. Carobbi had a highly successful career as a player. He was a defender in the great Milan side coached by Arrigo Sacchi in the late 1980s, playing alongside the likes of Marco van Basten, Ruud Gullit,  Frankie Rijkaard and Franco Baresi. Around this time he also played for the national team. After Milan, he played two seasons for Fiorentina before ending his playing career at Lecce.

Carobbi, who is a Category 1 Professional Coach of the Italian soccer federation, spent five years coaching in the Soccer School of Pistoia Nord before joining Fiorentina in 2003. He has worked with the U11s and the U13s and this season was asked by Corvino to take over the U15s.

The session which follows, from November 2007, lasted about 80 minutes and was structured around four elements: technical work, a possession game, tactical work, and a final match.

3.50pm Technique and warm-up
The first technical activity, lasting 10 minutes, served also as a warm-up. The 22 players were divided into five groups of four with one pair. Two players in each group took up fixed positions with another two, opposite, about 2-3 meters away, swapping positions.

The fixed player would serve the ball to his opposite number who would return it in a variety of ways – on the volley, on the half-volley, with a control on the chest then a volley, on the thigh, with a header and so on. After each return, the player who has played the ball swaps position with the other "mobile" player. When he moves to the left of the square he returns the ball with his left foot, and with his right when he moves to the right. Every two minutes the couples switch position.

Carobbi walks up and down the line of players looking closely at each group, shouting key words like "precision". On the volleyed return he demands that the kicking leg is opened out wide, away from the body to get the right line of return when kicking through the ball, and the arms are used on either side for balance. Carobbi gives continuous encouragement to the players when the skill is correctly executed. On the headed return he demands quick movement of the feet in the cross-over move once the header has been made.

4.05pm Possession, man-marking and warm-up
The players then play an 11v11 possession game in an area about 40m x 30m with two goals made from poles on each side. The players pass the ball by hand and have to finish the move with a header into one of the two goals. Every player is man-marked. The club believes that defenders have lost the ability to mark and that this is a fundamental defensive skill. Carobbi wants to produce Italian-style defenders. Defending players have to intercept the ball by reading its trajectory, rather than ripping the ball from the hands of the opponent in possession. Every couple of minutes the game is stopped for a minute of stretching. The game is designed to be fun but with technical requirements.

4.15pm Tactics: 8v4 and 6v4
The group is divided into two: half the boys go off for fitness work, the other half remain with Carobbi for two tactical exercises. In the first exercise, the

players are split into attackers and defenders with a goalkeeper on one half of a full-sized pitch. The defensive line is organized in a flat back four. They face four attackers and four midfielders, both starting off playing in a straight line.

Carobbi stops the play after one minute to point out that with a two against one advantage the attackers should already have scored. Although, ostensibly, the purpose of this is to put pressure on the forwards to speed up the play, there is a hidden psychological agenda: he is trying to boost the confidence of the back four. The back four tries to push up whenever possible to compress the play but the offside rule is not used. This is also for psychological reasons: if the defense were to get their timing wrong several times in a training session they would be inhibited from pushing up during a match. Much of Carobbi's focus is on the positioning and movement of the defenders. He wants them to keep the right distance apart, with the players pulling right and left in a chain, not squeezing up too closely together so as to leave space for a switch of play out to the other win, and not getting pulled so far apart that they invite a quick through ball for one of the attackers to move on to.

Carobbi calls for more communication between the players saying that there is no place on a soccer pitch for silent people. He wants the attackers, when taking on an opponent in a 1v1 to get up close to the defender before making his move. After 10 minutes he stops the session for some more stretching.

The second activity is a 6v4, plus a goalkeeper. The attackers are organized into a 2-3-1 formation, which matches the formation used by the team in competitive matches. The move begins when one of the two "holding" players plays it forward, usually to the middle of the three more advanced players who is operating as a kind of playmaker. He either knocks the ball out wide and moves in for a return pass or looks for a one-two with the center forward. Once he has received the ball back, he looks for the ball which will get a team mate into a dangerous position, either through the middle or around the back of the defense.

When there is no obvious forward ball, the playmaker has to keep possession, passing sideways or backwards, looking for one-twos, before attacking again. The striker should look to pull the central defenders back towards the goal while looking for the opportunity to suddenly come short for the ball from the playmaker. When he makes his forward move beyond the back line, he should attack the space between the two central defenders.

The timing of the players' movement off the ball is critical. Carobbi stops the play several times when a forward goes either too early, which would risk getting him into an offside position, or too late, giving the defender the chance to close him down. However, Carobbi leaves it up to the player where to move, which space to attack. He doesn't want the players to memorize schematic attacking moves and then to repeat them, like soccer robots, but to have a repertoire of possible solutions and to use their own initiative according to the situation.

He tells the defenders not to double up on the wide attacking player. They are already outnumbered, if they put an extra man on one forward they will be exposed elsewhere. Carobbi wants the forward players to move the ball around quickly. After a few minutes he imposes a two-touch rule to speed up the passing.

4.50pm Match
A match with two full teams in just over half of a full-sized pitch for 20 minutes. The game is played two-touch. Due to the restrictions on space and time, the match is played at a fast pace. Carobbi wants the players to play with courage, holding up the ball even when under intense pressure, and wants a high level of aggression but without getting carried away in the tackles and risking injuring a team-mate.

Exercises

Exercise 1

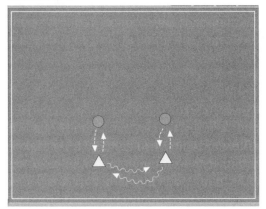

Organization: Players split into groups of four, with two opposite pairs. One pair is fixed, the other mobile, with the two mobile players switching positions right and left. Each fixed player serves the ball to his opposite number who returns it.

Variation:

The ball is returned in a variety of ways, changing every minute or so, from a half volley, a full volley, a header, a ball played off the thigh, and so on. The couples switch roles every couple of minutes, so everybody serves and everybody returns.

Exercise 2

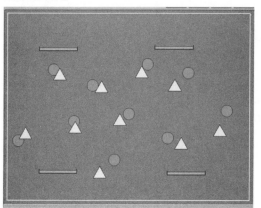

Organization: The players are split into two teams in a space about 40m wide by 30 long, with four small goals made from poles. The ball is passed by hand and the move must finish with a header on goal. Every player man-marks his opponent.

Exercise 3

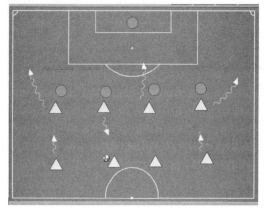

Organization: Four defenders, lined up in a flat back four, plus a keeper, take on eight attackers.

Coaching: The defenders must keep the right distance apart, moving right to left as a unit and compressing play where possible. They must not double up on wide attacking players. The attackers must move the ball around quickly, looking for spaces through the middle or around the back of the defense.

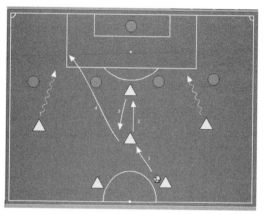

K+4 v 6

Exercise 4

Organization: Four defenders, lined up in a flat back four, plus a keeper, take on six attacking players who are in a 2-3-1 formation.

Variation: One of the two deep midfielders plays the ball into the middle of the three forwards who then looks for a way to get a ball through the defense, either for the wide players to attack or for the striker to run on to. The central striker should look to attack the space between the two central defenders.

Chapter 8

CESENA
Coaching the U15s, with Stefano Piraccini

"They're learning to play in team units"

AC Cesena, currently in the second division, has for many years been way ahead of most of Italian soccer in nurturing young talent. "We are unique in Italian soccer," says youth set-up coordinator Roberto Biondi, "in that here the success of the youth set-up helps to finance the first team, whereas in every other club it is the other way around."

Stefano Piraccini

Cesena probably rivals Atalanta as a production line of talented young players, many of whom go on to play for big clubs. Top goalkeepers like AC Milan's Sebastiano Rossi and Inter Milan's Alberto Fontana, along with Italian national team players like midfielder Massimo Ambrosini from AC Milan and Lorenzo Minotti, who captained Parma in the 1990s, all learned their trade at Cesena. In the 2005-06 season, 11 of Cesena's first-team squad were products of the youth set-up.

Some of Italy's finest coaches have also started here. Arrigo Sacchi, who would later lead AC Milan to European Cup glory, won his first trophy in soccer with Cesena's U20s in 1982, while World Cup-winner Marcello Lippi spent two years as first team coach.

Secrets of success
There are three secrets to Cesena's success. First, the club is economically stable – it has had only three owners since it was founded in 1940 – and so it is able to think long term. Second, it has a wide and sophisticated network dedicated to the

observation and recruitment of young players, for which Biondi is responsible. Third, it has a high standard of coaching. In each group, the chief coach works closely with both a specialist fitness coach and a skills coach.

Below, Biondi explains how the youth set-up functions, while Stefano Piraccini, coach of the U15's, takes a typical two-hour session with the help of skills instructor Ivan Zauli. The team trains three times a week and plays a match on Sunday.

Get them young

Cesena recruits about 30 youth-team players every season, many of them around nine or 10 years old. "We like to recruit boys as early as possible, because the years between 10 and 14 are the most important. If we can get the kids when they are young, they will be more receptive to the way we work. The thing we look for above all else when recruiting a youngster is good technique," Biondi says. The club has 16 talent scouts, enjoys a "sporting collaboration" with 32 amateur clubs in the region of Emilia-Romagna and has good relations with many others, which allows the club to have first pick of the area's most talented youngsters.

The club also gives great attention to the pastoral side of coaching. "It's vital that the youngsters are not uprooted from their families so, with some rare exceptions, we only choose boys who can return home at the end of the day." The club maintains close links with the schools which the players attend and if a player is performing poorly at school, he may be excluded from training to give him time to catch up. As Biondi puts it, "school comes first, then soccer. If they are dedicated at school, if they become responsible boys, then men, they can also achieve important results in sport."

Control and move: warm-up

The two-hour training session, with 24 players, is based on controlling the ball at various heights, from various trajectories, using different surfaces of the foot, in such a way as to allow the player to move away with the ball. The session is divided into technical exercises, with repeated drills, and match-play situations.

The first activity is a warm-up and an introduction to the ball control skills which will later be practiced more

Control and move

intensely. The boys are split into two groups of 12, and in each group three boys take up position at one of four markers positioned in a diamond. Player A strikes a firm pass along the ground to player B, who controls it and turns away to pass to player, C, who repeats to player D. The players vary the activity using different parts of the foot, first the inside of the foot, then the outside, first with the right foot, then with the left foot. The player receiving the ball has to control it in such a way that he can turn away from the passer in the direction of the next player.

The players seem to be having more difficulty in controlling the ball with the outside of the foot, especially as the practice pitch is hard and the surface bumpy. Technical instructor Ivan Zauli keeps reminding them to keep their toes raised as the ball arrives, if the foot is kept too flat the ball will bounce over it. However, if the ball arrives above the ground they should raise their heel and keep their toes pointed down.

After the warm-up the boys split into two groups of 12, with Zauli handling more technical drills and Piraccini working on match-play situations.

Pass and overlap

In Piraccini's first activity, three players with one ball run across the pitch, from one touch line to the other, inter-passing and overlapping. The player in the middle passes to one of the players on his outside, and then moves wide to overlap the player who has received the ball. The move is repeated at high speed until the players arrive at the other side. "It is a simple activity but the speed is important. The team plays a match on Sunday, so often on Friday we work on speed in preparation for the match."

Pass and overlap

The activity is not as fluid as it should be and Piraccini quickly picks up on what's going wrong. "The player receiving the ball needs to know where he's going to pass to, so he has to take a look at where his free team-mate is positioned. Today quite a few of them are getting it wrong. Either they are looking up too soon – things on a soccer pitch can change completely in the space of a second – or not looking at all. The time to look is just before the ball arrives at your feet."

103

6v6 – playing in units of three

Piraccini takes 12 boys and splits them into two teams of six, playing in one third of a full-sized pitch with four small goals. The attackers can score in either goal. Six players – three attackers and three defenders – operate in one half of the pitch and six in the other. As a variation, the pitch is split by a vertical line, rather than a horizontal line.

"The key to the activity is for them to get used working in units, in a small chain of three players, but there are many different team-play aspects involved: everybody attacks and everybody defends, they have to think about the timing of their movement without the ball, and the timing of runs to lose a marker, they need vision to see the right pass, and they need to execute the control-and-move techniques, practiced earlier, to keep the play moving." Piraccini wants all the boys to be involved, even when the ball is not in their area, through their movement. He rarely stops the play to give instructions but instead shouts key words to players, such as "active" or "participate".

Sensitivity

Piraccini says that one of the keys to working with boys of this age is to recognize that it is a time when players can experience a rapid physical development which is not always accompanied by the same rate in mental development. "You can find that you suddenly have a player in a man's body but who is still really in a pubescent phase. So you have to be sensitive in the demands you make on the players. Those players who don't grow as rapidly can struggle physically at this stage and that can be demoralizing. But the smaller ones who stick it out become better players because they have to learn ways to survive and adapt against players who are bigger and stronger."

Control drills

While Piraccini works with 12 boys, Zauli takes the other 12. In Zauli's drill, the players are divided into pairs. One player stands in the middle of a square, about 5m x 5m, of four markers; his partner stands outside the square, about 5m away. The partner throws the ball towards the player in the square, who has to control it first time. The variations are constant: control with different surfaces of the foot, with both feet, with the ball thrown at different heights and at different speeds. Then further variations are added. Instead of just controlling the ball, the player in the box controls the ball and moves outside the square to pass the ball along the ground to his partner.

As in the earlier exercise, Zauli focuses on the shape of the foot in the moment that the ball is received. When the ball is being controlled from a height, on the outside of the foot, for example, he reminds the players to angle their foot with the toes pointing downwards. He also corrects the body posture of the players receiving the ball, making sure that the back is kept straight with the knees thrust slightly forward, as the ball is being delivered.

As a development, Zauli takes eight of the boys and plays a game of 6v2, in a square of around 8m x 8m. The "attacking team" has one player stationed permanently at each corner of the square, leaving the other players in a 2v2 in the middle of the square. Every player has to use two touches on the ball, one to control the ball and one to pass. The attacking team tries to put together 10 passes. The technical requirement is similar to that of the earlier exercise: control the ball in such a way as to open up play. But now it is under the pressure of an opponent and the player in possession has to make a very quick decision as to the choice of pass required to keep the move flowing.

Exercises

Exercise 1

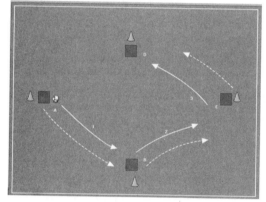

Organization: Four markers in a diamond, with a player at each marker. Player A passes the ball hard along the ground to player B, then continues his run to the second marker. Player B controls the ball and turns towards player C, and continues his run to the third marker, and so on.

Variations: Use both the inside of foot and the outside of foot to control the ball. Use both feet to control and pass.

Coaching: Crisp, accurate pass along the ground; open body shape which allows the receiving player to control the ball and move away towards his target; 180-degree vision; when controlling with the outside of the foot position the foot according to how the ball arrives: if it arrives flat along the ground keep toes up, if it's bouncing, raise the heel and point the toes downwards.

Exercise 2

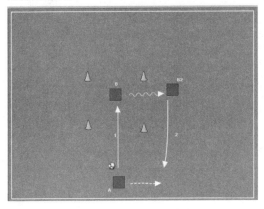

Organization: Four markers arranged in a square, two players. Player A stands in the middle of the square, player B outside it about 5m away. Player B throws the ball to player A, who has to control it first time.

Variations: Use both the inside of foot and the outside of foot to control the ball. Use both feet. A controls and moves outside the square, then passes along the ground to B.

Coaching: Vary the trajectory, height and speed of the thrown ball so that each control requires a slightly different movement; receiving player keeps back straight and legs slightly bent, with knees thrust slightly forward.

Exercise 3

Pass + overlap.

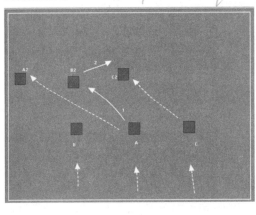

Organization: Three players, one ball, playing cross the pitch from touch line to touch line. The players all set off running at speed. The central player (A) passes to one of the two outside players (B or C) and then overlaps him. The player now at the center, passes to the other wide player and then overlaps him.

Variations: Use both feet.

Coaching: Keep the speed up; the receiving player must look to see where his wide team-mate is just before he receives the ball.

Exercise 4

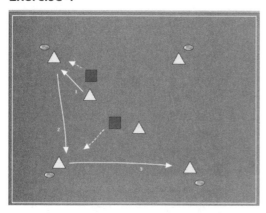

Organization: Eight players, 6v2, in a square. One "attacking" player is stationed at each corner, two are free in the middle but are marked by two defenders. The attacking team must complete 10 consecutive passes to score a goal. Every player must take two touches on the ball, one to control and one to pass.

Coaching: Quick choice of pass; good body shape to control the ball in a way that opens up the play; central attackers look to slip marker to be able to play give-and-go balls.

Exercise 5

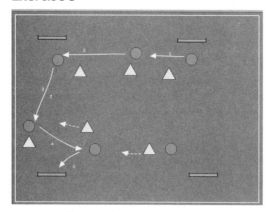

Organization: 12 players, 6v6, in one third of a full-sized pitch, four small goals, two at each end. The pitch is divided into two by the penalty area line. In each half of the pitch there are three forwards marked by three defenders. Players can score in either of the opponents' goals.

Variations: The pitch is divided by a vertical line instead of a horizontal one.

Coaching: Attack and defend in units; vision – look all round for right choice of pass; make a quick decision on choice of pass; good body shape to control the ball in a way that opens up the play; right timing of runs to slip marker; give-and-go balls to slip marker.

Chapter 9

BOLOGNA
Coaching the U13s, with Michele Borghi

"The calling card of every young player is how he strikes the ball"

Bologna FC 1909 is one of Italy's most successful clubs, having won the "scudetto" – the Italian championship - seven times. However, the last title win came in 1964 and in recent years the club's ambitions have been more geared to reaching one of the Uefa Cup places. At the time of this interview, in 2004, the club was in Serie A but at the end of the 2004-05 season was relegated to Serie B.

Michele Borghi

Bologna doesn't make the headlines as often as AC Milan or Juventus but it has been, in many respects, one of the most forward-thinking of Italian clubs. Giuseppe Gazzoni, Bologna's main shareholder until the beginning of the 2005-06 season, was one of the first Serie A presidents to understand that if clubs spent more money than they earned they would not survive for long. From the late 1990s onwards he refused to sign star names on huge salaries, focusing instead on nurturing home-grown talent.

Small but dynamic
There are seven youth teams at Bologna and the youngest group – the U13s – are in hands of Michele Borghi. The group is made up of 21 players. The team plays in a regional championship against kids aged 12 and 13. Michele explains that the club deliberately put together a group of boys who were on the small side but dynamic and with decent technique and put them in a league with slightly bigger boys to push them and prepare them. "They are at a disadvantage physically at the moment but we hope that next year they will be stronger for the experience."

The approach

At Bologna the emphasis is on getting the basics of technique right from day one, Borghi explains. "We don't spend a lot of time on tactics with the U13s. Lots of technical work on the basics and lots of match practice are the key elements. We prefer to have a small number of technical and individual tactical objectives and work intensely on those rather than trying to cover everything more superficially."

"For the youngest boys the most important technical aspect is passing and receiving. The calling card of every young player is how he strikes the ball. Many youngsters these days come to clubs lacking in the basic ability to pass and control the ball. I do talk to the players about tactics but it is always from an individual point of view: if I am a defender how should I position myself when the other team is attacking? If I'm attacking, what position should I take up to be able to receive the ball? We don't get into structural team tactics beyond asking for a basic level of organization and positional sense during games. When they move up to the U15s they will begin to learn a bit more about tactical issues."

Both feet

"Using both feet is fundamental. We hammer home this principle from the very first day. When the players arrived at the beginning of the season, they were a bit behind in this respect because they hadn't been used to using both feet. I'm pretty satisfied with the progress they have made. Apart from one or two players who still struggle a bit with their weaker foot, they have all improved a lot."

Mentality

Borghi says that for a youth coach winning isn't everything. How the team plays is more important than the outcome. "When I started out in coaching I used to enjoy watching the team play to win. The longer I spend working with youngsters, the more I realize that winning is not that important. Your team could win a game in which the players have made lots of individual errors and the problems get masked by the victory. You could lose a game but notice that many of the players have made important improvements and that is more satisfying than winning. The secret of being a good youth coach is being able to identify and correct defects in the players. When they get into the U15s and U17s winning becomes more important."

Structure: a typical week

The boys train in two-hour sessions on Monday, Tuesday, Wednesday and Thursday, with a match on Saturday. Each session is based on four phases after an initial warm-up activity: 30 minutes of technical exercises, 30 minutes of themed, small-sided matches, 30 minutes on further technical exercises or working on match-play situations (1v1, 2v1 etc), 30 minutes for an open match.

110

Each week is based on one of the fundamentals of technique and each day of the week is based on a specific element of that technique. "This week is about passing, so one day is all about passing with the inside of the foot, one day for passing with the inner part of the instep, one day for passing with the full instep, one day for passing with the outside of the foot."

Today's session: passing with the inside of the foot

The first group of passing and receiving exercises begins with the players working in pairs and then in groups of four in an 8m x 8m square. Each exercise is brief - four to five minutes - and repeated with variations that ensure that all players have to use both feet, all have to pass the ball both forward and diagonally, and that all have to pass and receive while standing still and while in movement. The level of difficulty and intensity is gradually increased throughout the phase.

"There are a variety of things I am looking for. I want them to look up when they have controlled the ball and to time the pass correctly. With the diagonal pass, the players have to think about which foot to use. If you are standing still and playing a forward ball, you can use either foot. But if your team-mate is moving and you have to find him with a diagonal ball, you have to choose which foot to use and he has to choose what body shape to adopt when receiving the ball."

Michele Borghi makes a point

After half an hour the players are split into three teams of seven. They play on a small pitch with half-sized goals. Two teams, A and B, play against each other while the players of team C take up positions along each touchline. They will act as a "sponda", or support, for the players in team A. Players in team A can only touch the ball three times. The players in team B have no restrictions. There are three games of about ten minutes with the teams switching roles, so that each team gets to work with the support players.

The activity is based on the give-and-go techniques they have been practicing and on improving tactical awareness. "The free team tries to attack directly and can use as many touches as they need to get past their opponents. The players with three touches will often find their path blocked by an opponent. They can't dribble him so they have to make a choice: look for a forward pass or use the support players to the side. If they can, they should look for the forward pass, but if not they should look for support – this way they get used to using the whole width of the pitch to keep the ball moving. This is about tactical awareness but it is also linked to the training exercises because to use the support players properly they have to execute the give-and-go moves they were practicing earlier."

The players then go back to the squares for more technical work on passing and receiving. The exercises expand the give-and-go elements that were introduced briefly earlier but are more demanding and Borghi demands that they are executed more quickly. For the last 30 minutes, two teams play a free match, with no restrictions, in a three-quarter length pitch with half-sized goals. Borghi does not stop the game but makes comments to players during the game regarding their positioning or choice of pass.

Communication
Borghi's explanations are short and sharp and always accompanied by a short demonstration. Some parts of the session require a very hands-on approach. "In the exercises and the themed games, I get in close to the activity a lot to hammer home the technical and tactical points which are the object of the day's session. I rarely intervene in the open match. What I ask from them in the match is intensity, so there's no point me stopping the game every few minutes with instructions. After an afternoon of hard technical work you have to leave space for them to express themselves and to explore."

As far as possible, he keeps the mood of the group upbeat and positive. "Sometimes it is necessary to say 'that's not the right way to do it' but if kids at this age hear you yelling all the time 'you've done it wrong – you've made a mistake' they can get a bit upset so I always try to make criticism constructive, explaining with positive examples and encouragement."

Stretching
Boys of this age don't need to spend a great deal of time on fitness and stamina work. Instead, every ten to fifteen minutes, and in the pauses after matches, they do a couple of minutes of light stretching, concentrating on the legs. As Borghi explains, this has several functions: "It gives them a brief rest between demanding exercises and helps to calm them down a bit so they can listen properly to the explanation of the next activity. But it also increases their flexibility and mobility which helps them to improve the technical execution of passing and receiving."

Exercises

Exercise 1

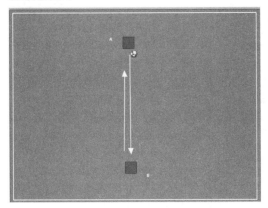

Organization: Players in pairs, 8m apart, exchange passes. Pass and control with right foot, pass and control with left foot, control with left and pass with right, control with right and pass with left.

Coaching: Keep the body shape open to react to arriving ball. Position the standing foot wide of the ball while playing the return pass. Keep the kicking foot solid and at right angles to the direction of the pass.

Exercise 2

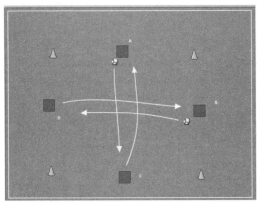

Organization: Four players in a square 8m x 8m, divided into two pairs. A passes to C, B passes to D, each player controls with one foot and returns with the other, always using the inside of the foot.

Coaching: The players have to look up before playing the ball to avoid the two balls clashing in the middle and have to think about the timing of the pass.

Exercise 3

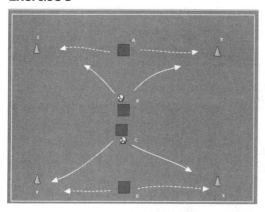

Organization: Four players, divided into pairs in the same 8m x 8m square. B passes to A who returns the ball first time while moving along the line. B controls the ball before returning. At point x, player A returns the ball with the right foot, at point y with the left foot. C and D do the same. After 4/5 minutes players switch roles

Coaching: The player receiving the ball must keep his head up and watch how and where the ball is arriving.

Exercise 4

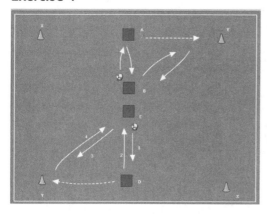

Organization: The same four players in pairs in 8m x 8m square. All players are stationary. B throws the ball to A, who returns it with inside of foot on the volley, first with right foot then with left foot. C and D do the same. Then A and D move along the lines, returning the ball from point x with the right foot and from point y with the left. After 4/5 minutes the players switch roles.

Variation: The whole exercise is repeated with the ball returned on the half volley (first stationary, then in movement).

Coaching: Feet with heels slightly raised to allow greater reactivity. Watch the flight of the ball to time the pass.

Exercise 5

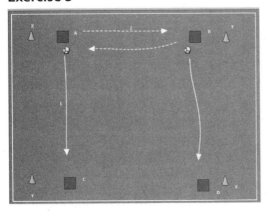

Organization: The same four players in pairs in same 8m x 8m square. A passes to C and at the same time B passes to D. A and B then change places, C and D stay in position, so that C returns the ball to B and D to A. The player at point x always stops the ball with his right and returns with his right, at point y always uses his left. After 4/5 minutes, the players switch roles.

Variations: A begins with a diagonal pass to D, and B to C, before A and B switch sides. A begins with a straight pass to C who returns a diagonal ball towards the space where A is arriving.

Coaching: The players have a tendency to play a sloppy pass because they are already on the turn as they play the ball and so have the wrong body shape – the pass must be executed with total concentration before the player moves. Players are receiving the ball on the move so must keep their heads up to watch the ball arriving. When playing the diagonal ball the players have to think about the timing of the pass.

Exercise 6

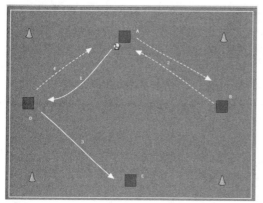

Organization: The same four players, the same square. A passes to D and then moves to where B is standing, B moves to where A was standing. D must then play a diagonal pass, either to B (in A's old place) or to C, switching position with the other player in diagonal (so if he passes to C, he changes places with B). The player receiving always controls the ball first before playing the next pass. Once the basic rules are understood the exercise must be played at a fast pace.

Coaching:

For each pass, one of two players could receive the ball so both have to keep alert with the right body shape. The pass can go either left or right so the passing player has to choose the correct foot to play the ball, using his right foot to play to his left and vice versa. The direction of the "go" movement is no longer automatic, it could be either left or right depending on where the ball has been played, so players are having to make quick decisions and movements.

Chapter 10

Parma

Coaching the U13s, with Filippo Fabbri

"Control the ball to open up play"

AC Parma was one of the most successful teams in Italy in the 1990s. Backed by the wealthy Tanzi family, the club bought some of the world's top players like Juan Sebastian Veron and Hernan Crespo. But when the Tanzi dairy company, Parmalat, crashed in 2004, the club was left with huge debts. AC Parma folded and a new club, FC Parma, was created.

Filippo Fabbri

Despite the club's difficult financial position, the youth set-up has remained strong. The exodus of many top stars gave youth players a genuine chance of breaking through to the first team, which is the most powerful motivational factor for a young player. Former youth-team players like Alessandro Rosina and Tonino Sorrentino were in the first team squad in the 2004-05 season, when the club provided 12 players for the youth sides of the Italian national team.

What is immediately striking about the coaching at Parma is that, from the youngest players through to the stars of the first team, there is a unity of approach: on every pitch you can observe similar activities, all based on a small number of core principles. Gabriele Zamagna, who has been head of the club's youth set-up for six years, explains how those principles were developed. Youth coach Filippo Fabbri demonstrates how they are put into practice with an U13 group.

Anticipating the crisis

Zamagna said that the club had observed the general economic downturn in soccer and in 2001, well before the Parmalat crash, and had reacted to it. The club appointed Luca Baraldi as director general at the same time as coach Arrigo Sacchi moved "upstairs" to become technical director. The new approach was to attract and develop talented young players who were struggling to find a regular first-team place at other clubs and to invest more in developing local youth players.

Sacchi made his name as the coach of the great AC Milan team of 1988-91. His attacking soccer was something of a revolution in a country where defensive soccer was the order of the day and although he later left to become sporting director at Real Madrid his influence is strongly felt at Parma. "When Sacchi appointed me to run the youth set-up he gave me clear directives about what he wanted," says Zamagna. "The three core activities are: individual ball skills, possession of the ball as a team and giving team play a direction."

Structure

While each coach has some autonomy in how to run an individual session, the club does have a standard training session structure which is applied at every age group. This involves 30 minutes of work on individual technique on the ball, 15 minutes on keeping possession of the ball as a team, 20 minutes on match-play situations like 1v1 and 2v1, a 20-minute themed match with restrictions, and a final 30 minutes for a free match with no restrictions.

One of the most common possession activities used by Parma at all levels is an overload situation, such as 8v4. This type of activity is very hard work for the team defending and trying to close down the space but, Zamagna says, it allows the attacking team to build up a large number of touches on the ball which helps build confidence. "If you try possession games in numerical parity it is very difficult. The team in possession rarely gets more than two or three touches before the ball gets intercepted and the move breaks down. With overloads like 8v4, the team with the ball can consistently put together moves of 10 and 11 passes while still under the pressure of an opponent."

Right atmosphere

The training sessions are intense but Zamagna says that it's vital they take place in the right atmosphere, without too much pressure. "One of the key things about Parma is that we try not to transmit tension to the coaches and technical staff or to the players. In order to make it as professionals, the players have to develop the right technical abilities but our work goes much deeper than that. First we try to develop the person with the right values who can play a full role in society, second the soccer player. Winning at all costs is not our philosophy although, of course, we try to win and have had some success. We want players to play with enthusiasm and to represent Parma as a brand and as an institution in the right way."

Ball skills: control and turn

Filippo Fabbri's session with 12 players from the U13 team takes place on a seven-a-side pitch with a synthetic surface. It begins with an activity based on individual ball skills, lasting about 12 minutes.

Coach Fabbri gives advice

The players are split into groups of four, with each player beginning at the corner of a square of around 15m x 15m. Player A carries the ball a couple of steps in the direction of player B. He passes the ball along the ground to B and continues his run so that he ends up at B's corner. Player B, meanwhile, controls the ball with the inside of his foot and turns at the same time, heading towards C. He also takes a couple of steps towards C before passing the ball along the ground and continuing his run. C repeats with D, who is then facing an empty corner. Rather than passing, he feints to pass, then carries the ball to corner A where he stops. As a variation, the drill is repeated in a clockwise direction, with A passing to D, D to C, and C to B, so that the players have to use their left foot to control the ball, run with it and pass.

"What I'm looking for here is the kind of ball control which enables a player to open the game up. You don't stop the ball so that it goes back in the same direction or kill it so it stays still but control it so that you can turn away with the ball in one smooth movement. As well as the basic control technique with the inside of the foot, you need 180-degree vision so that you can see both where the ball is arriving from and where you want to be heading once the ball arrives."

The most common technical error in this exercise, Fabbri says, is that the player receiving the ball adopts the wrong body shape. This is typically due to the non-kicking leg being positioned incorrectly or being too rigid. When this happens Fabbri gets in to demo a more open, flexible body shape at a slight angle to the passing player.

Possession: 8v4

Fabbri's second exercise, which lasts about 15 minutes, is based on group possession with an overload, 8v4. A rectangle about 40m x 20m is divided into four areas, with the players divided between the four areas so that in each quarter there is always a 2v1 situation. Neither the attackers nor the defenders can move out of their zone. In the attacking team, one player from each zone takes turns to move into

Parma 8v4

the middle of the rectangle so that the other attacking players always have an option to play through the middle. However, the player doesn't leave his own zone. The defenders are changed every four to five minutes until everybody has had to attack and defend at least once.

The exercise puts into practice, under the pressure of an opponent, the principles of the first exercise: controlling the ball in a way that opens up the play and passing along the ground with the inside of the foot. Fabbri says that dividing the pitch into zones limits the players' movement but is necessary. "Being still quite young, there is a natural tendency for the players to congregate in the area of the ball. The way to teach them that that the ball will still arrive even if they are a long way away is to force them to stay in their area. In earlier versions of this activity they were fixed to a precise position, not just a zone."

Fabbri demands that the ball is moved around at high speed and frequently intervenes if players dwell on the ball too long or make the wrong choice of pass, such as trying too long a pass when a short ball was available or playing the ball to a player very tightly marked when another player had more space. He also asks the supporting players to make runs within their zone to make it easier for the player in possession to find them. "There are many different solutions for the player in position. He can wait for the defender to close him down and then try to dribble him or can draw the defender in and then play a one-two. Or he can just play a simple early pass to keep the move going."

Match situations: 2v2 with keeper

The next activity is a 2v2 attacking move down the center of the pitch which lasts about 20 minutes. To start the move, player A passes a diagonal ball forward to player B. B then attacks the space in the center of the pitch while A moves to his right on an overlap. Defenders at C and D move forward to close down the attackers. One goes to the man on the ball, the other tracks the support player.

There are several variations which altogether last another 20 minutes. The first variation is that player A begins ahead of B and starts the move by passing a diagonal ball backwards, so when B attacks, A is already ahead of him. Another variation is to remove one defender and try similar moves with 2v1, focusing more on a fast attacking overlap and shot. Each drill is repeated with the attackers beginning the move on their left foot.

Fabbri wants player B to attack his defender and where possible to beat him in a 1v1, using his support player only if necessary. "Within the 2v2 situation the quickest way to goal is if the attacker can dribble his player and get in a position where he has a clean shot at goal. But the next best solution is to try to create a 2v1 situation in which the attackers can play a quick one-two which also opens up the space for a shot. So what I'm looking for is the player carrying the ball to show some courage and fantasy in taking on his man, and to attack him at high speed with his head up and for the wide player to choose the right time and direction of movement to support him."

Support options

Fabbri outlines the various options open to the support player in a 2v2 situation. "For example, when my team-mate has the ball and is unmarked and I am behind him, I should make a wide overlapping run, to take a defender away or to give him an outlet for the pass. If he is closed down, I should come in close to support him. If I am ahead of the ball and my team-mate has the ball and is unmarked, I can make either a diagonal run to open up a pass for him or I can pull back to support him and give him a short pass option. If he is closed down, then I should move into a position where we can play a one-two."

Several players are reluctant to dribble the defender and quickly opt for a pass to the support player. Fabbri explains why this happens and how he deals with it. "Twelve-year olds have a strongly developed sense of themselves and their own limitations. Those who are aware that they possess the right technique will take on their man and will enjoy it but those who feel that they are less gifted technically are more inhibited and reluctant to try. They need to be pushed and sometimes I exaggerate the demands I make on them to get the point over."

Finish with fantasy

Fabbri also demands that the players finish off the move properly. Some of the players seem to feel that the job is done when they have beaten their man and they relax when they get in front of goal. Fabbri continually tells the main attacker to get a real strike on goal and for the support player to follow up the shot in case the keeper spills the ball. "I want them to finish with a shot but I don't criticize them if they make a mistake in this part of the activity. It's important that they feel that they can be creative in front of goal and try something different. We all like to watch players of fantasy like Ronaldinho, so they must have some space for experimentation."

Match 6v6

The session finishes with a 6v6 match with one rule: for a goal to be valid all five outfield players have to be in the opponents' half when the ball goes in the net. "It's an old rule and maybe a bit clichéd now," Fabbri says, "but it's still useful to help keep the team compact." On other days there are themed matches with varying restrictions but today's session has been very demanding physically and Fabbri decides to give the players more freedom. "You have to always remember the purely ludic aspect of playing soccer and allow them to have some fun. They cannot be expected to have the same level of concentration at the end of a session as they did at the beginning."

Exercises

Exercise 1

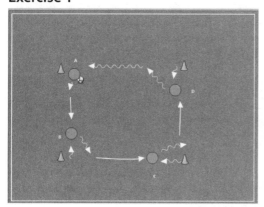

Organization: Groups of four players, four plastic markers make a square about 15m x 15m. A carries the ball forward a couple of paces and then passes the ball along the ground to B, and carries on running to occupy the space at marker B. As A starts to move, B moves a couple of paces towards A so that when he receives the ball the space between the players is reduced to about 10m. B controls the ball with the inside of his foot and in the same movement turns back towards the marker and then changes direction and heads towards C, once he has passed to C he continues running to occupy the space at marker C. The action is repeated with C taking the ball and passing to D. D is then heading towards an empty marker point, so rather than passing he feints to pass and then carries the ball to marker A and then stops.

Variation: The activity is repeated in a clockwise direction, with A initiating the move by passing to D and so on, so that each player has to both pass the ball and stop the ball with his left foot.

Coaching: Players must control of the ball well with the inside of the foot and turn away from the direction of the

122

passing player, keeping a good open body position which allows a 180-degree view of the pitch. Players must pass the ball accurately along the ground with the inside of the foot. Players carry the ball forward using the outside of the instep. The last player must carry out a convincing feint of pass.

Exercise 2

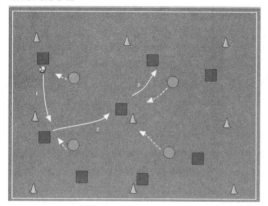

Organization: 8v4 in a 40m x 20m rectangle divided into four areas, in each section there is a 2v1. The attackers have one player who stays in the middle. The four defenders change places with four attackers every 4-5 minutes.

Coaching: Good first touch essential to control ball and open up play. Crisp passing along the ground with inside of foot. Support players move off the ball must help player in possession. High tempo: don't dwell on the ball unnecessarily. Use feints and one-twos to open up space. Pass to the closest team-mate wherever possible.

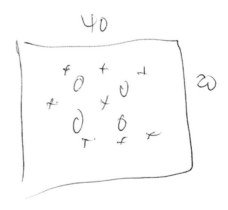

Exercise 3

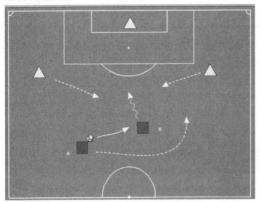

Organization: 2v2 using the full length of a 7-a-side pitch, with a keeper. A passes the ball forward to B, who then attacks the goal down the center of the pitch, A then goes wide to the right in support. A either beats his man and shoots, looks for one-two and shoots or tries to put B in a position where B can shoot.

Variation: A starts ahead of B and begins by passing the ball back to him 2v1, focusing on a wide overlapping run by the support player. All repeated with players using left foot.

Coaching: **Attackers:** Dribble at speed and show imagination to get past defender. Play one-twos to create space. Support player makes diagonal runs to take away second defender. Support player makes wide overlapping runs.

Defenders: One player goes to close down and one covers. Both try to intercept the pass.

Chapter 11

INTER MILAN

Coaching the U11s, with Giuliano Rusca

"Touch, awareness, speed and dialogue"

FC Internazionale Milano, founded in 1908, is one of the three clubs which has dominated Italian soccer in the last 40 years, along with Juventus and A.C. Milan. Inter has won the Italian league title 15 times, the last time in 1989, and won the European Cup twice in the 1960s. The club was awarded the league title in 2005-06 after disciplinary measures against league winners, Juventus, and runners-up, AC Milan. Inter also won the 2006-07 title.

Giuliano Rusca

Inter has invested heavily in developing its youth set-up and is now beginning to see the fruits of that investment. The U20 'Primavera' side won the Italian Cup in March 2006, beating rivals AC Milan in the final, and in June 2006 the U15s won the national league title, beating Bari in the play-off final. Former youth-team players like Nigerian striker Obafemi Martins and defender Marco Andreolli broke through to the first-team squad.

Giuseppe Baresi, head of the club's youth set-up, says that Inter's philosophy is "to develop the youngsters in the most complete way as soccer players in order to help them make it into the first team as young as possible. At the same, we want to help them to develop personally, to help build their character so that they can fit into society and into the world of work and to help them to be able to relate to other people in a world outside that of professional sport."

Selection for the U11s

Inter's youth set-up is made of two U20 teams – the 'Primavera' and the 'Berretti', two U17 sides, two at U15, two at U13 and three at U11. The club draws on four Soccer Schools within the city of Milan, where there are full-time Inter staff members, a national network of 60 soccer schools called "Inter Campus", which are Inter-branded franchises, and a team of observers who watch teams across the Lombardy region.

The four local Soccer Schools (to which access is open to all children between six and eight, regardless of merit) have over 300 children in total. The best two or three each year make it to the U11s. The Inter Campus network has about 2,000 young players up to 17 years of age and provides around 30-40 per cent of the total intake of Inter's youth set-up. Boys from outside the region of Lombardy can only be signed once they have reached 14 years of age.

Becoming more business-like

The youth set-up at Inter is currently in a period of self-analysis in line with the desire of club president, Massimo Moratti, to make it a profitable arm of the club in its own right. This is partly due to the general desire of Italian clubs to be more cost-effective and partly in response to the new regulations of Uefa, European soccer's governing body, which compel clubs to have a quota of locally-trained players in the first-team squad.

Baresi: "It's about being more professional and better organized, which is a stimulus for us to always improve the quality of our work. It's a sign of the importance that the club places in the youth set-up. They are prepared to spend to develop young players but they also expect a return on that investment. The Uefa rules will strengthen youth set-ups. Maybe, at the beginning, a handful of the really big clubs contested the Uefa rules but that was because they are the ones who are always capable of putting their hand in their pocket and buying the top players. Maybe these rules will help to close the gap between the really big teams and those below them."

Club line and competitive spirit

"There is a clear club line about how work should be conducted. For example, we like to play with a back four because that is how the first team plays. We like the first part of the training session to be individual technical work and the second part to be based on applied technique, which involves the beginnings of tactics. Then there is a physical element, especially with the older boys, which in today's soccer is increasingly important. Within this framework each coach brings his own abilities, ideas and methods."

"In being able to get across the importance of the right result and the right way of playing, without exaggerating the demands placed on the younger children, much depends on the personality of the individual coach or instructor who has to communicate the culture of winning and how to win. It is important even for the youngest children to achieve something, whether it is learning how to keep up the ball a certain number of times, or beating a team-mate in a sprint, or beating the opponent in a practice game or a competitive match. But you need to arrive at this competitive spirit by degrees. If you push too hard too soon you will end up with the kid who wants to win so badly that he cheats, or spits at opponents or swears at the referee."

Individual skills and specialization

"When there is too much emphasis on the result there is a risk that coaches will overlook the work needed to develop the players' skills on an individual basis and focus entirely on coaching team units and the team as a whole. Coaches are professionals, they are paid according to results so this focus on results is to some extent understandable but you can lose out on the quality of some of the players. So we communicate to our coaches the importance of developing individual technique. I want to create a program to try to restore this kind of work, which would mean more work with the individual players and less with the whole team. I am convinced that if you have 11 high-quality players the team will win on its own, without needing to spend hours learning about pressing and team tactics."

"I had a conversation with one of my coaches recently about this. I asked him: what is the identikit of the ideal defender? He replied: someone who is tall, strong, good in the air, fast, who knows how to tackle and how to mark. So I asked him: how many of these characteristics do you work on? We work very little on heading. There is very little work specifically on developing speed. Nobody works any more on challenging, tackling, slide tackling and so on, because everybody is so worried about getting a yellow card. So how can we produce a quality defender if we are not teaching him these things? We have to take two steps back and remember how to construct the player so that maybe we can take three steps forward in the future."

"Part of constructing the player is choosing the right player to specialize in a particular role. Often you have players who can play in three or four different roles, who can perform all of them to a standard of six out of ten. I would prefer to develop a player who knows one role that he can perform to a level of eight out of ten. You can have 11 players who know how to do everything to a reasonable level but who will never play for the first team at Inter. But if I have one right back who can play to a high level, he might make it through."

The right kind of coach

"At Inter, we believe that coaching the U11s is just as important as coaching the first team. We give the same importance to all levels. It depends, of course, on finding the right coach for each age group. It's no good having an U11 coach who does his job with an eye on moving up to the U17s or U20s. He wouldn't do the job properly. If you can get someone who is genuinely satisfied by working with the U11s, he will communicate the right ideas to the boys."

Giuliano Rusca, coach of Inter's U11s, is exactly the kind of coach that Baresi had in mind. Rusca has built a career on working with boys of 6-12 years, including a nine-year spell at AC Milan alongside Fabio Capello, who later won league titles with Milan, Real Madrid, Roma, and Juventus and is now England coach. Rusca has written several well-known books on developing this age group.

Surprisingly, perhaps, given his success, Rusca plays down the significance of the role of the coach, pointing out that in a professional club like Inter, the initial selection process goes a long way to determining the kind of results the youth teams achieve. "You have to start with talented kids. A coach can make a difference along the way but at least 60 per cent of what makes a soccer player is innate. Soccer skills are not part of our genetic make-up but the propensity for a certain type of athletic activity is. When choosing boys to come into the U11s we look at two things: the kind of relationship the player has with the ball and the way he resolves match situations, with and without the ball. And we give precedence to players who can do things quickly."

In the 2005-06 season, the Inter U11s category was made up of over 60 boys aged between eight and 11, that is, boys born in 1997, 1996 and 1995. Each year has its own team and plays in a separate league. The A team, the oldest, plays in a regional league; the other two, the B team and C team, play in local leagues. The A team is coached by Rusca and Fabio Pesatori, the B team by Davide Aggio and the C team by Bruno Casiraghi and Gianni Vivabene. Manuel Amoroso is the goalkeeping coach for all groups. The children train three times a week for two hours. One of the sessions, on Wednesday, is voluntary but most boys attend.

Training session

At one training session in March 2006, the players were split into five groups of around 12 to 16 boys each. The goalkeepers worked partly with Amoroso and partly with the other groups. Each coach works with his own team during the season and Rusca rotates during the week to work with each group at least once. The other coaches work primarily on developing individual technique while Rusca works on match play, which covers everything from 11v11s down to 1v1 situations.

The A team (10-11 yrs): small-sided matches

Rusca oversaw several small-sided games, which were either 4v4, with no keeper, or 5v5 with a keeper, in a pitch of 30m x 30m. Each player had an unlimited number of touches in his own half but in the opposing half had only two or three touches. "This way there is little time in the finishing phase and more time in the build-up phase," Rusca explains. "There has to be a feeling of safety in the build-up but precision and speed in the finishing phase, both in the first touch to control the ball and in the shot on goal or cross. It's about technique applied in a situation of limited time and space."

Rusca stopped the games several times to talk to the players. "Today I was trying to communicate the importance of precision in all aspects of the play, from a good first touch to a safe and effective pass. When I stopped them it was usually for a technical error but also for their tactical choices, like the choice of pass. They were looking all the time to pass wide whereas I wanted them to try to pass through the middle, vertically. These are the kinds of aspects we are focusing on in this period, which is part of a program for the season. Earlier in the season we did a lot of work on possession of the ball and then work in the final third where the players can take greater risks by dribbling. In this way, you gradually transmit the concept to them that they have to build the play in a certain way until the final third and once in the final third they have to conclude the action in a certain way."

The A team: 3v2 with overlap

On the pitch next to Rusca, Pesatori prepared the A-team boys not involved in the game with a series of technical and tactical exercises. First, they spent 30 minutes juggling the ball with various parts of the body. Then they conducted a series of exercises in squares of four players based on passing, receiving and movement off the ball. "This group is involved in technical work but also work on the kind of passing and movement which is related to match situations," Rusca explained.

The session ended with a tactical exercise based on using an overlapping wide player in a 3v2 attacking situation (see Exercise 1). Three forwards took on two defenders plus a keeper. The central forward, player A, played the ball to his team-mate on the left, player B, and then moved wide left to overlap him. Player B attacked the goal, with player A wide to his left and player C wide to his right. The object was for player B to go straight for goal and try to score and to use the wide players only if he needed to. The two defenders began the exercise stationed in wide positions and only once the first pass had been made from A to B could they move infield and try to challenge the attackers. The main focus of Pesatori's attention was the movement of attackers A and C off the ball. He pointed out the wide players were tempted to come in centrally to help player B but that this only made the job of the defenders easier, as they had less space to cover. By staying wide, they split the two defenders and opened up space for B to shoot. As soon as one defender moved to close down the shot, he left space for one of the attackers.

The B team (9-10 yrs): ball skills, passing and movement

On a separate pitch, Aggio coaches a group of 16 boys in a variety of ball skills ranging from ball-juggling to crossing and shooting. In the first activity, a square is created with four poles with tape connecting the poles at a height of about 30cm (see Exercise 2). The boys first had to run through the square passing the ball under the tape, jumping over the tape, and carrying on out the other side, moving the ball along with a combination of touches with the inside of the foot and the outside of the foot. Then they had to run through while juggling the ball, jumping the tape and making sure that the ball didn't hit the ground. They could juggle the ball using any part of the body. "That area is a minefield," Aggio shouted, "don't drop the ball."

Inter players juggling the ball through the square

The players were organized in four lines of four, each arriving from a different side of the square so that four players entered the square simultaneously. In this way, each player had to concentrate not only on keeping control of the ball but also in avoiding a collision with another player. There were then a series of variants. First, each player entered and then turned right at 90 degrees before exiting. Later, two players entered at a time, one juggling the ball before passing it to his team-mate on exiting for the latter to have shot at goal. The players then moved on to a sequence of crossing and finishing moves playing the ball off a forward target man to a wide player before moving into the box to finish.

"The essence of these activities is improving the relationship a player has with the ball in all ways – running with the ball, juggling the ball, passing and shooting. The objectives are purely technical. This is part of a micro-cycle of 10 days work in which the coach has to cover all of the technical skills of soccer," Rusca says.

The C team (8-9 yrs): running with the ball

In one half of a five-a-side pitch with a synthetic surface, eight boys practice ball skills while the other half of the group plays a match on an adjacent five-a-side pitch. Later, the two groups will swap over and the session will then end with a match involving all the boys.

In one of the technical activities, Vivabene created four adjacent squares with four plastic markers (see Exercise 3). Inside each square, there were two boys. First of all, the boys had to move around without touching the ball and avoiding contact with their team-mate. Then they had to dribble the ball around inside the square, always avoiding contact with the team-mate. On a cue from the coach, the players had to kill the ball, leaving it in the square, run to the next square in an anti-clockwise direction and start dribbling around the balls in that square. Vivabene demanded a high level of concentration from the boys, as eight-year-olds typically have limited attention spans. He asked the players to move the ball rapidly and precisely, using many soft touches on the ball and to react quickly to the cue to change squares.

On the next pitch, Casiraghi oversaw a match between the other players. He stressed the importance of not all congregating around the ball. "The intelligent player is the one who can find himself some space to do something important," he told them. At one stage, he stopped the game as a player in an advanced position was calling for the ball from a defender. He asked the boy whether it was easy for the defender to reach him with the ball over that distance and what the forward could do to help. The boy realized that he needed to find some space towards the center of the pitch to make the passing distance shorter for the defender.

Speed

One of the most noticeable aspects of the activities with all the groups is that the coaches demand that the exercises are carried out at high speed. The message is repeated time and again to the boys. "Speed is something which has to be developed because a skill is performed within a given space and time and the faster they are, the more effective they are in a match. If you have talented kids they will adapt to this. There is no evidence that if you first learn something at a low speed you can then gradually increase the speed and eventually perform the same skill at a high

At Inter, speed is stressed

speed. It is more likely that if you learn skills at high speed you will be able to reproduce them at high speed. We have traveled a lot to big clubs around Europe, like Ajax and Manchester United, and this is now how everybody thinks in the important youth set-ups."

Difficulties

Rusca described one common problem: "We have noticed that the difficulty which nearly all our kids have is the play after the first touch on the ball, which is usually a control touch. What to do next is a problem. It is a problem of sensitivity to the ball and also a problem of making the right choice. So we work hard on the precision and quality of the first touch because this conditions what happens afterwards. In all the technical exercises we insist upon this."

Roles

"Usually the kids have their own motivation to play in a particular role and that certainly makes things easier for us. Sometimes, we intervene by giving them advice on what role might be suitable and asking them to play in a different role. We also get the younger boys to try out various roles, being aware that this a phase in which exploration is important. It enables us to see the child's aptitudes and enables the child to develop in different ways."

Dialogue

With all the groups, even the youngest there is a continuous dialogue between coaches and children. The coaches frequently asked the players questions like: Why did you make that pass? Why did you pass in that moment? What were the alternatives? What do you think would have been the best choice?

"This dialogue is a choice we have made for this age group. We intervene to give directions on how they should play. It's a way of making the boys take responsibility for the choices they are making. Ultimately, it's the boys who have to play the match, not the coaches. We can't play the game for them but we can make them think about what they are doing, so that they begin to ask themselves the same questions on the pitch. On the pitch they have to think and think quickly. The player has to be able to make an effective choice in very limited time if he wants to have a future in soccer."

Exercises

Exercise 1

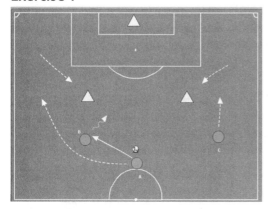

Organization: Six players in a small grid, about 30m by 20m, with one goal. Three attackers versus two defenders and a keeper. The three attackers begin in a line with player A passing the ball to his left to player B. A then moves wide to overlap B on the left, who comes inside to attack the goal. Player C moves wide to the right. The two defenders start on the two touch lines and can only move in to defend once the first pass has been made from A to B.

Variations: The overlapping run is made on the right hand side of the central striker.

Coaching: B has to shoot as soon as he has a clear sight of goal and only passes to A or C if he is closed down. A and C have to create space for B with the timing of their runs and create space for themselves if B is closed down and needs to pass. A and C must not get sucked in towards the center when supporting B. The moves must always be conducted at high speed.

Exercise 2

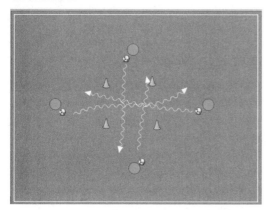

Organization: Four posts are placed in a square and are joined by tape at a height of about 30cm above the ground. The goal is about 25m away. Players line up on all four sides of the square. Four players, one from each side, have to enter the square simultaneously with the ball under control and exit out the other side.

133

Variations:	The ball is juggled through the square using various parts of the body. The players make a 90-degree turn inside the square to exit at right angles to the direction they entered. Two players enter at a time, one with a ball, one without. The player with the ball juggles it, and as soon as the two leave the square he passes it to his team-mate who shoots on goal.
Coaching:	Juggling with delicate touches to keep the ball close to the body. Observe the movement of the other players to avoid a collision. Everything must be performed at high speed.

Exercise 3

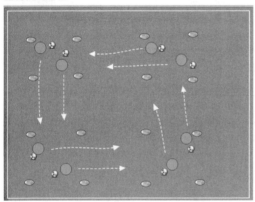

Organization: Four squares are created using four colored markers for each. Two boys per square. The players guide the ball around inside the square. At the coach's signal, the players leave the ball and move to the next square in an anti-clockwise direction.

Variations:	The boys move around inside the square, without touching the balls, before switching squares. They switch squares moving in a clockwise direction.
Coaching:	Players must concentrate fully on the activity. Lots of quick, soft touches to keep the ball close to the foot. Keep head up when guiding the ball to avoid a collision. Rapid switch between squares.

Part 4

Sharing knowledge

Chapter 1

Developing soccer intelligence in young players
The Sportilia Stage

"Children's low attention span is an alibi for bad coaches"

In addition to the recognized coaching badges of the Italian soccer federation, a number of courses are run throughout the year by the federation, by local coaches' associations and by clubs. In recent years, one of the most popular and most successful has been the "Stage for Youth Soccer Coaches."

The 'Stage', or course, is run by the Emilia-Romagna branch of the National Coaches' Association (AIAC), in conjunction with the Italian soccer federation. It is held every spring at Sportilia, a modern multi-sports complex in beautiful surroundings in the hills near the border between the regions of Emilia-Romagna and Tuscany.

The fifth edition of the course was held in May 2006. For the first three years, 2001-2003, AIAC invited coaches from Atalanta to run the technical and tactical sessions. From 2004 to 2007, they are run by coaches from Inter Milan. The guest coaches in 2006 were: Massimo De Paoli, coach of Inter's U15s; Angelo Pereni, a highly-experienced club coach and Vincenzo Pincolini, one of Italy's top fitness instructors.

Stage 2006: soccer intelligence
Each year, the course is dedicated to a few core elements of coaching for a particular age group. The 2006 course was entitled "The Development of Soccer Intelligence in Youth Soccer: How to Coach the Application of the Fundamentals of Technique and Tactics" and focused mainly on the 10-16 age group.

The philosophy of the course was explained thus:

"Every instructor of youth soccer must always bear in mind in the choice of exercises which make up his weekly program and yearly plan for training, the following aspects:

- the level of knowledge and ability of his team
- the way his team defends and attacks
- the individual abilities of his players
- the way the opponents play

"Soccer is a game of situations and of collaboration and therefore the growth of the young player has to be based on applied technique and individual tactics, which are the cornerstones of collective tactics. Soccer is taught and is learned through playing and the knowledge of combinations between two or three players represents for the young players a behavioral patrimony which can be drawn upon to provide rapid choices to problems of play during games."

"In the development and growth of a young player, the ability to analyze the game and to know how to take adequate initiatives are predominant factors, therefore the instructors must propose in training sessions a large number of tactical solutions for the attack and the defense. This will help to improve the capacity for concentration, attention, and collaboration, factors which are important for cultivating a strong team spirit."

The teaching took place over three days, beginning Friday afternoon and finishing on Sunday afternoon. It was divided into theoretical sessions in a lecture hall and practical sessions on the pitch. The sessions included: fitness preparation for 6-10s and 11-14s; coaching technique for 10-16s; the physical development of the young player in the U15s; coaching individual tactics for 10-16s; coaching ball possession by the team and by team units; coaching the offensive transition; and counter-attacking at high speed.

Massimo De Paoli's "Castle", is an example of how the two kinds of teaching (theoretical and practical) were integrated. De Paoli is widely regarded as one of Italy's top youth coaches – his U15s at Inter won the national title in 2006 – and he is also in demand as an instructor of coaches for his ability to communicate his ideas with clarity and enthusiasm. He is the type of public speaker who would be a millionaire if he dedicated his life to the circuit of management motivation conferences. Instead, he prefers to talk soccer.

De Paoli's introduction to his coaching session was typically offbeat. He had been driving down to Sportilia from Milan on the Friday afternoon, he said, when he saw a sign for the city of Sansepolcro, home to the Italian Renaissance artist Piero Della Francesca. Instead of stopping at Sportilia, in the region of Emilia-Romagna, he headed on down to Tuscany to spend the afternoon admiring Della Francesca's work.

"I had prepared a load of slides to show you, explaining various tactical schemes but looking at Della Francesca's paintings made me think about the power of the imagination and how important it is to coaches working with youngsters. It's no good reading coaching manuals if you are not prepared to give your heart and soul to the coaching of children. Youth soccer coaches always have to ask themselves: what motivates me as a coach? Is it a career? Is it rivalry? Is it wanting to show that I know best?"

So instead of a slide-show lecture, he would describe a game called "The Castle", using it to explain how soccer tactics can be taught to young players in way that captures their imagination. It was based on a very simple idea and was communicated using a small number of key words. The most important thing, De Paoli said, was for the coach to really visualize in his mind the imaginary world he was describing and to make the players see it too. Poles would be used to represent the 'guardians' of the castle. Plastic markers would create the 'gateways' into the castle. If the young players were made to 'see' guardians and not poles, see gateways and not plastic markers, they would perform the activities with a greater degree of motivation. It all comes down to the capacity of the individual coach to inspire, to make players see what he or she sees. "It's no good practicing a 3v2 if we are not able to create the perceptual framework which enables players to really see the numerical advantage."

Most coaching manuals will tell you that younger players have a low attention span and that this should be taken into consideration when planning coaching sessions, but De Paoli warns that "the low attention span is often used as an alibi by coaches. If the attention of young kids is waning it is because they are not motivated and that is usually down to poor communication. Young kids love soccer, they dream about soccer and if you can get on their level and tap into those dreams you can motivate them."

Conquering the castle: how to attack space
The 'castle' to be conquered is the space between the opposition's midfield four and the back four – the most vital space on the pitch in the construction of attacking plays. The key words were: castle, gateway, blind zone, width, depth, short and long. The gateways are the spaces between the areas in which opposing players operate and through which the right kind of pass has to be found. The blind zone is the area beyond the opposing back four in which a player will be offside if the ball is played forward to him. Width means spreading

the ball horizontally and depth means getting it forward vertically. A short pass is one which is played to the feet, a long ball one which is played in front of a player who is in movement.

Four poles are placed in a line across the pitch about 4-5 meters apart and about 4-5 meters from the edge of the penalty area. These represent four defenders. Another four poles are placed in parallel about 10 meters further forward, towards the half-way line. On either side of each of the eight poles are two plastic markers, each about one meter away from the pole. This meter represents the defender's area of activity, i.e. the distance he would be able to stretch to intercept a pass. Four midfield players are lined up facing the first row of poles. A further four players are stationed close to the defensive poles, with their backs to goal. The two wide players will operate as opposition full-backs closing down the wide midfield players. The two central players operate as attackers.

The activity is developed sequentially (see diagrams). In the first part of the exercise, one of the wide midfield players advances along the flank and is blocked off. He turns and plays the ball backwards, from where it is moved quickly along the line to the other wide midfield player. The players are being guided in using the full width of the pitch to find alternative points of attack. De Paoli emphasizes that all of the four players are continually active, even the three who don't have the ball, because they are continually adjusting their position in accordance with where their team-mate in possession is moving.

So, for example, as the wide midfield player (Player A) moves up the flank, his nearest team mate (B) moves across to cover him, the other central midfield player (C) moves across but drops a meter or so deeper, while the other wide midfield player (D) slides across in line with Player B. When A is blocked off and switches the movement with a pass to B, the ball is moved from B to C (B may carry the ball forward a few paces before laying it back to C) and then on to D and the line of players makes exactly the same covering movements but in reverse.

Throughout the exercise the two forward players take it in turns to make runs towards the player in possession, one coming short and then dropping back, then the other coming short. De Paoli points out that a great deal of the work of a forward lies in continually making yourself available for a pass which frequently doesn't arrive. It's easy to see when the player is beginning to get frustrated with the lack of service. Either he stops making the runs or he starts complaining to his team-mates. The great forwards, he says, are those that will make those runs for 90 minutes knowing that the right pass only needs to come off once to create a goal-scoring opportunity.

140

The young 'warriors' have tried to take the castle from the side but have been repelled. They have to keep the ball and find another way in, this time through one of the gateways. Instead of looking for width, moving the ball horizontally along the line, they will go for depth, attacking through the middle. This time, when one of the attackers comes short, and calls for the short pass (to his feet) he will be served with the ball. Because the striker will be marked, nine times out of ten he will probably be unable to turn and attack the goal, so at first the forwards look to lay the ball back to one of the two central midfielders. In both cases, the forward pass and the lay off, De Paoli wants the ball to be played accurately along the ground bang in the middle of the two plastic markers – if the players don't 'see' the gateways, the pass will be less accurate.

In the final part of the exercise, one forward comes to receive the ball, the second forward gives him a shout that he is unmarked and instead of laying the ball back he turns and finds his team mate with a pass. Now the two forwards have got the ball in the heart of the castle and they have to get out the other side to score. There are a number of options. If his team mate calls 'long', the forward in possession can play an immediate through ball bisecting the two central poles, for the second striker to run on to. Or the second striker can come towards the ball and look to play a one-two, putting the first striker in with a ball behind the defense. As before, the pass through the defensive space must be accurate and correctly weighted, the pass and the run beyond the back line must be timed so that the receiving player does not move into the 'blind zone' too early (thus being caught offside) and the move must be finished with a decent strike on goal.

"The Castle"

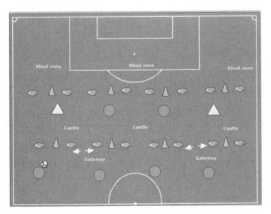

Organization:
In one half of a full-sized pitch, four poles ('guardians') are placed horizontally across the pitch, 5-6 meters apart. Four more poles are placed in line with the first set but just beyond the goal area (the space between the two sets of poles is the 'castle'). On either side of each pole, about 1m away, is a plastic marker (the plastic markers between each set of poles create the 'gateways'). Four players are stationed between the half-way line and the first set of poles, four players just in front of the second set of poles.

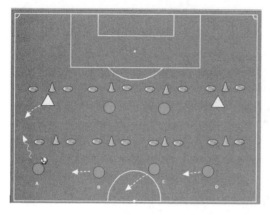

Build up

The move begins with player A taking the ball into a wide area. As player A moves wide, player B moves across, player C moves across but also moves backwards a few steps, and player D moves across. Player A is furthest forward, players B and D on the same horizontal line and player C is behind them. As player A takes the ball forward he is closed down by the wide player opposite.

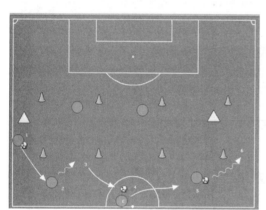

Option 1

Player A turns back towards his team mate, and hits a pass to player B. B either takes a couple of paces forward and passes to C or passes straightaway. C passes to D who looks to take the ball forward in the wide right area. These horizontal movements, left to right and right to left, are then practiced for 4-5 minutes. All the time the ball is moved along the line of four players, the two central attacking players, E and F, take it in turns to make runs towards the player with the ball.

Option 2

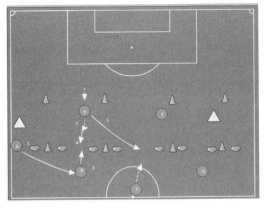

When player A is cut off, he turns and plays the ball to B. B has two options: he can move the ball along the line to C or look to play a ball into the feet of one of the attackers who has come short to receive it (he calls 'short'). When E first receives the ball he assumes he is tightly marked to plays the ball back immediately to either B or C. When B and C receive the ball, they have the same options: continue to move it along horizontally or look for a short ball forward. These movements, alternating vertical forward and backward passes with horizontal passes, are repeated for 4-5 minutes. All balls forward and backwards (into and out of the 'castle') must pass through the 'gateways'.

Option 3

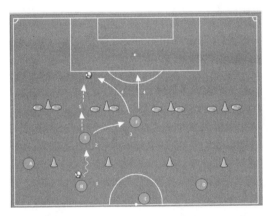

When player E has the ball, his team mate F, can choose to let him pass it back but now can also call for a pass. When F calls for a pass, he comes in short, player E turns and plays a hard early ball along the ground to his feet and then makes a run towards goal. F has two options: he can turn and attack the goal or he can look to play a one-two with E and then attack the goal. The timing of the runs beyond the last line of poles must be correct to avoid being caught offside. The move should be finished with a convincing strike on goal. All balls forward and backwards (into and out of the 'castle') must pass through the 'gateways'.

Chapter 2

The disappearance of the man-marker: reasons and remedies

"Young players are in trouble defending in a 1v1"

When Italy won the World Cup in 1982, defender Claudio Gentile gave a master class in man-marking. Italy had many players to thank for their victory: Paolo Rossi for his goals; Dino Zoff for his Zen-like calm between the posts; and Marco Tardelli for his tireless running and powerful shooting. But Gentile was the key. His man-marking of Argentina's emerging star Diego Maradona, of Brazil's elusive playmaker Zico, and of West Germany's tricky winger Pierre Littbarski laid the foundation of Italy's triumph. But as the 1980s wore on, almost every Italian team switched to zonal marking and the figure of the great man-marker disappeared.

Every year at Italy's Viareggio youth tournament some of soccer's biggest names come to discuss important aspects of the game. The 2006 technical conference, organized by the Italian soccer federation, was dedicated to one of the basic skills of soccer: marking.

The starting point of the conference was a comment made in 2005 by Italian World Cup-winning coach, Marcello Lippi. Players just don't know how to man-mark anymore, he said. Is this true? If so, why? And what can be done to remedy the problem?

Trying to answer these questions were: Lippi himself; Azeglio Vicini, president of the technical sector of the federation and Italy coach at the 1990 World Cup; Antonio Rocca, coach of Italy's U16 and U17 sides; and other federation experts.

Azeglio Vicini: The problem of marking was rightly raised by Marcello Lippi in one of the meetings of the federation's technical committee last year. It has become evident in recent years that players don't know how to mark. It's not just a question of zonal defense versus man-marking. It's about when to mark, where to mark and how to mark. How often these days, even at the highest level, do we see attackers scoring a goal from three yards out, completely unmarked? Why does this happen? We should ask whether in training sessions, even for young players, marking should be taught as a basic skill.

Marcello Lippi: Every soccer nation has its own traditions and it is right that they should try to preserve something of those traditions. When I talk about Italian soccer, I am talking about the national team. You cannot talk any more about clubs as representing a country's soccer culture.

One of the characteristics of Italian soccer, in the days when it was successful, was the ability to defend and construct counter attacks. Italy, in those days, produced great defenders – I don't need to list all the names. Italy's last great results [the World Cup victory in 1982] happened at a time when there were great defenders. But in the 1980s we started trying to learn from other countries and one of the effects of this was a greater emphasis on the athletic side of soccer.

We still have great defenders in Italian soccer but they are not specialists at man-marking. They are great defenders within the context of the team unit. It's easier to teach zonal marking to players than it is to teach man-marking. If you go to see players being trained you will see lots of beautiful training sessions but you will never see individual players being coached in how to mark. Youth coaches from the U15s upwards should start looking at how to incorporate defense into their sessions.

It's natural that there should be emphasis on forward play. As a club coach, I spent around 80 per cent of my time on coaching forward play but that was also because I inherited many defenders who were already "made" – they already knew how to defend.

Antonio Acconcia, (Italian soccer federation, coordinator of the federation's school for coaches): In the 1980s, Arrigo Sacchi had great success as the coach of AC Milan using a zonal defense. Until then, almost everybody used man-marking and a sweeper. After Sacchi, everybody switched over to zonal defending and this filtered down even to the youth set-ups. All of the coaching, even of the youngest players, became conditioned by this. The coaching of zonal defending was based on the coaching of the defense as a unit and not thought of as part of the development of the individual player.

Attilio Maldera, (Italian soccer federation, responsible for the development of youth and schools soccer): There has been an excessive concentration on zonal defending at youth level in recent years and basic skills such as intercepting and closing down players have not been coached. Being a good

146

defender requires a number of abilities: positioning, temperament, timing and reading the game. Some of this ability is innate but some of it can be learned and therefore can be coached. So what kind of coaching do we need? First of all, there should be more analytical exercises [exercises in which the activity is broken down into its component parts, explained and demonstrated to players] before conducting situational activities and matches. It is also important to analyze defensive errors which were made in the previous game and to correct them in the next coaching sessions.

Antonio Rocca: It has been suggested that there is an inherent problem for the defender in zonal marking: he has to take on board too much information. Certainly, the role of the defender has become more complicated with the switch from man-marking to zonal defending. In the past, the role of the defender was to interrupt opposing attacks and to destroy their build-up play. This was his essential job and he didn't need to do much more. He would touch the ball maybe 20 times in a match. In the modern game, the defender might have 100 touches on the ball. He is called upon to control the ball and help build up play. The modern defender is half defender, half midfield player.

In evolving into this new role, the defender has gained some new skills and lost some old ones. Young players, between 14 and 18, struggle when they have to defend against a direct opponent. If you say to a young player, 'mark that man', he will look at you and say, "what do you mean, coach?". The coaching of individual defending has been abandoned, so a young player is in trouble defending in a 1v1 situation.

Behind this evolution, there is also a social dimension. As poor societies developed into rich societies, the role of aggression in the culture was modified and the physical aspect of play was diminished. The disappearance of street soccer is significant in this respect. When kids used to learn soccer in the streets they also learned life in the streets. I used to wonder why a city like Naples, which was richly creative in many other respects, always seemed to produce defenders rather than creative players. I once asked [Parma defender] Paolo Cannavaro about this and he said: 'from the age of five, if you don't know how to defend yourself in the streets of Naples you will get beaten up.'

Developing aggression was necessary as a means of overcoming obstacles in life and also, possibly, as a means of overcoming a sense of inferiority. Today's kids don't need that. Life is planned out for them in such a way as to remove as many obstacles as possible in advance and to eliminate competition.

Despite all these factors, there are still kids who want to be defenders. What is interesting is that, when you talk to them, they want to be central defenders – either sweepers or stoppers. The full back is on the road to extinction. What is the reason for this? One reason is that coaches increasingly want big strong lads in their teams. The typical center back is big, strong in the air, rhythmical in his movements but without a quick sprint and sometimes lacking in coordination. The typical full back was always small and fast. Nowadays, because of the lack of natural full backs, many teams convert wingers into full backs. These players tend to be good in the build up play but not so good in winning the ball back.

Renzo Ulivieri, (former coach of Bologna FC and president of the Italian coaches' association): A defender once said to me in the old days, 'if an attacker gets past me, I won't be able to put dinner in front of my kids." In those days, defending was a means of survival. Man-marking was very difficult. You didn't always have the sweeper to cover and you had many 1v1 situations, so you had to know how to deal with that.

When Lippi and I started coaching, everybody was moving to zonal defending but we were lucky because we inherited a generation of players who had learned to man-mark. To take a player like this and teach him zonal defending is easy. It takes three days or a week. But if you take a kid who has only ever learned to play zonal defense and try to teach him to man-mark, it's very difficult. Having said that, if zonal defending was taught properly, it would give players a basis in marking.

When looking for a solution to the problem, it is important not to assume that zonal defending is the opposite of man-marking. We were taught three key reference points for defending: the goal, the opponent and the intention of the player in possession. To mark, you don't need to be physically attached to the opponent.

Much of the coaching in modern zonal defending is based on protecting the defender from being exposed to a 1v1 situation – ultimately it is the tactics of how to avoid defeat. Players always double up on the opponent to protect the last defender, so the defender doesn't get used to dealing with 1v1. There are two remedies. One is using more small-sided games. If you play 7v7 you don't have the numbers to be able to double up all the time on attackers. The other is simply coaching players how to defend 1v1. Coaches should not be ashamed to do this. There are three basic principles. (1) Positioning: the defender should be close enough to touch his direct opponent. (2) Body shape: he should be on his toes, with his knees slightly bent, ready to pounce. (3) Timing: he has to know when to attack the ball and when to hold off.

There is much debate about whether marking should be gradually tighter the closer the opponent gets to your goal, so that the players in your penalty area are marked the most tightly. I think that this is open to discussion. For me, the really great defenders know the right distance to keep and it is a knowledge which is based on understanding exactly what kind of attacker they are facing.

148

Daniele Bernazzani, (U20s coach, Inter Milan): The decline in defending is part of a wider decline in technique. Much of this is down to the disappearance of street soccer and this cannot be reversed. It is true that coaches spend much more time coaching team units rather than individual players but this is because every youth coach is under pressure of time and, at U20 level, under pressure to get results.

Antonio Bongiorno, (responsible for the youth set-up at Margine Coperta, a feeder club in Tuscany for Atalanta): Many coaches are embarrassed to ask their teams to man-mark because they think that it looks negative and destructive. There are loads of great ex-defenders out there but how many clubs take them on to help coach youngsters in the art of defending?

Part 5

Laying the foundations

Chapter 1

Stefano D'Ottavio, head of the technical sector for youth and schools soccer, the Italian soccer federation

"Quality of teaching can replace quantity of spontaneous play"

Professor Stefano D'Ottavio is the man responsible for mapping out the technical development of youth football across Italy, covering all levels from amateur to professional. Every year, his department publishes the guidelines for how each youth category should be coached. It also publishes a very detailed book called A Technical Guide for Soccer Schools. This guide is the "bible" of youth soccer coaching in Italy.

Below, D'Ottavio talks about some of the most important aspects of youth coaching – such as the importance of speed and the use of small-sided games – and also talks about some aspects which are often overlooked, such as using the right kind of equipment for safety and didactic variety.

Technical decline exaggerated
It is frequently said by people involved soccer that the technical level of young players now is lower than it was 10, 15, or 20 years ago. The disappearance of street soccer, the reduction in school games and the increase in alternative forms of leisure are usually cited as key factors in this decline.

D'Ottavio, however, is far from pessimistic and thinks that talk about a major decline in technical ability is exaggerated. "Children are not less gifted naturally than they used to be. Social and environmental circumstances mean that there is less space and less opportunity for motor activity than there was 15-20 years ago, but time spent in Soccer Schools can go along way to reconstructing didactically that which children once learned on their own outside. Quality of teaching replaces quantity of spontaneous play."

Motor skills

"Work on motor skills and coordination, especially in the early stages of a player's development, is extremely important. It's vital that the training activities are rich enough to involve all of the child's abilities. From the quality and quantity of initial motor experiences the child develops his skills, which will be more flexible and suitable to the modern game. Working on technique without working on motor skills and coordination is like building a house with no foundation."

Small-sided games

"In the last few years in Italy, we have forced through changes to the rules so that players up to the U11s play small-sided games in small pitches. From 12 and 13 onwards the pitches start to get closer to regulation size. We believe that it would be much better to continue with this gradual approach until they're even older but it starts to get difficult for organizational reasons."

"There has been resistance to small-sided games in Italy to but we are overcoming it with studies, with information, with exchanges of knowledge. Later today at Coverciano, for example, we start a three-day refresher course with 100 qualified Italian FA youth coaches from the whole country, so that they can take our ideas back to their regions. Every regional FA then has a system of checks to verify that the new ideas are being implemented. It works, but it could always work better when you are talking about reaching a huge number of people. It could work better with greater investment. But the feedback we get back from clubs is positive."

"I have data from across Europe and South America and I would say that around 60 to 70 per cent of countries are moving in this direction. There is resistance but you have to push ahead. You need to be able to convince people with solid research not just opinions. The relationship that we have between the national coaches' association, the federation's technical center at Coverciano and the federation's youth sector is decisive in this regard. It's vital that three converge towards the same line because everything has to pass through the coach. If the coach is trained as a specialist youth coach, is well-informed and shares the ideas of the federation, everything is much easier in dealing with club officials, the children and their families."

Dribble and shoot

At a recent get together of Italy's youth teams, D'Ottavio noticed that there were two skills in which nearly all the players were weak: dribbling and shooting. "These were U15 and U16 players from top clubs like Milan and Juventus. They were fantastic at organizing the offside trap, at keeping the team compact and those kinds of things. But they didn't dribble and didn't shoot." He believes that young players no longer want to take risks because they have been inhibited by coaches who want to turn them, first and foremost, into team players.

"Shooting must be a key element in every coaching session, with at least 50 per cent of technical exercises – whether they are based on passing, receiving or running with the ball – concluding with a shot on goal. That's what everything builds up to in soccer, that's the conclusion, the end result. So it should be in training, too. When any two kids start kicking a ball around, sooner or later one will go in goal and the other will start shooting. Dribbling and shooting. That's what kids love."

Speed before accuracy

"A lot of people will tell you that when coaching young children you should first develop precision and then speed, but the opposite is true. There are studies which have been carried out in the US and in Holland which back this up. Even if they make mistakes, it doesn't matter: do it quickly. Children react very positively to stimulus based on speed and speed is the crucial factor in deciding whether someone will make it or not in soccer. If we can do the same things with a ball but I can do them more quickly than you, I'll make it and you won't."

"I privilege speed at all levels in coaching, even over accuracy which will come eventually. For a child to do something accurately, he or she has to pay great attention. This kind of attention to particulars is not a natural characteristic of young children. Our work must be adapted to their natural characteristics."

Never too young for tactics

"People make the mistake of assuming that tactics is about 4-4-2 or 4-3-3. Tactics is about something much simpler: choosing a way to behave. Choosing to cross instead of shooting is a tactical choice. So you bring tactics into work with even the smallest kids, when you suggest one way of doing something rather than another. With the younger players, I don't impose things on them but if I ask them to play, say, 4v2, I put in front of them a problem to which they must find the solution. I induce them to choose – that's tactics – and you can do this right away with kids."

"You should never tell kids what to do while they are playing a match. That's why the Italian federation has introduced time-outs during youth matches. The coach can talk to them for a minute and then they go back to play – but you don't want coaches yelling instructions at them during a game. That's wrong on all levels."

No fixed roles

"Young players should not have fixed roles or positions. In Italy, the U13s start to learn something about positional play which is then developed further at higher levels. But training should be a polyvalent learning experience, with players trying all roles. If I only ever play on the right side of the pitch, my brain and body become conditioned to reacting to the space in a certain way. Not only is it of vital importance to play in all positions but kids should be encouraged to play as many other sports as possible."

The right equipment
D'Ottavio is convinced that there is a fundamental aspect of coaching young children which is frequently overlooked: the equipment. D'Ottavio and the federation have been working for years with a company called Trial, a sports goods manufacturer in Forlì, in the north of Italy, to develop a range of sports goods designed to help every young soccer player to maximize his or her potential.

D'Ottavio believes that many Soccer Schools underestimate the importance of choosing the right equipment. In doing so, they are holding back their young players, or worse, putting them at risk. "The right sports equipment is necessary for two reasons," he says. "First, because the safety of the children is of paramount importance. Second, because variety is one of the most important stimuli for young children and the wider the range of equipment you have the more motivated they will be."

Trial president Bruno Montanari provides three disturbing statistics from Italian sport to stress the importance of using the right equipment:

☒ between 2002 and 2004, three children died during soccer coaching because heavy goalposts fell on them
☒ there are 161,000 outstanding legal actions brought by people who have been injured by defective sports or leisure equipment
☒ of children who abandon their first regular sporting activity, 27 per cent put the blame on shoddy equipment

Balls and goals
For D'Ottavio, the quality of the balls and the type of goals are two of the determining elements in any coaching session with young children. "We use balls of widely differing sizes. I believe that in the early phases of learning the ball should be a larger and lighter than normal. With a larger surface it is easier for the young child to make contact. Nearly everybody will tell you that it should be smaller."

The federation and Trial have developed a unique double-layered ball which feels a bit like a cross between a rubber soccer ball and a volleyball ball but has exactly the same movement and trajectory as a leather match ball. The balls are now being increasingly used throughout Italy with younger children, in girls' soccer, and – even at senior level – for practicing headers.
D'Ottavio believes that research into the health risks involved in repeatedly

heading a leather ball must be taken seriously. But he argues that safety initiatives such as the use of protective headgear in the USA are misguided. The simple solution, he argues, is to use a lighter, softer ball. "If you are you are wearing some kind of head gear, you are not actually heading the ball and so not developing the correct technique."

The goals must have the right dimensions for the anthropometric characteristics of the children using them and, crucially, must be safe. The federation and Trial have designed goals with an aluminum frame padded with rubber which have no sharp or protruding edges and which are light enough to be carried by the children.

Variety
On top of the two essential elements, balls and goals, there is a wide range of equipment which the federation recommends to Italian Soccer Schools to help enrich training sessions. One of the items which the federation and Trial have developed is called the "medusa" (also known as a 'wobble pad' or stability balance ball) because of its resemblance to a jelly fish. D'Ottavio explains its benefits. "It is sensitive to the joints and so helps to improve balance. It also helps to prevent injuries. If I create adaptations to irregular movements, my physical structure reacts and is strengthened, so it can take a greater strain. In soccer, you frequently have to react to things when you're off balance or have one foot off the ground and that puts greater strain on your joints."

The wobble pad has been so successful that it is now used by many teams in Serie A (Brazilian Ronaldo used it extensively while recovering from a knee injury in his Inter Milan days) but it is also great fun for children. Other products which D'Ottavio and Montanari have developed include a lightweight frame with a series of suspended weights, which can be used for activities ranging from the slalom to shooting practice, and a kind of elastic ladder useful for a variety of co-ordination exercises.

Session
D'Ottavio outlines how the equipment might be used in a typical 90-minute training session for U11s.

Phase 1: The first 10 minutes of the session should be "self regulating". The pitch is left full of equipment – everything that the Soccer School can provide – and the kids do whatever they want with whatever they find. The coach is present but stays in the background, not giving any instructions. This serves as a good warm-up and allows for exploration and creativity.

Phase 2: A period of 30 minutes with three technical and co-ordination exercises, all with a ball, which help develop reactions, balance, and combinations of movements. One exercise might involve, for example, player A standing on a medusa. Player B throws the ball to A, who returns it in a variety of ways (instep on the volley, inside of the foot on the volley, with a header).

Phase 3: The final 50 minutes should include a series of competitive situations like 1v1 and 2v2, or overload situations like 4v2, using small goals.

It's the journey that counts

Italy produces strong youth teams at both club and national level. However, D'Ottavio believes that too much emphasis is still placed on winning. "What counts above all is the journey from six to sixteen years of age and the development of the child at each stage." He makes the distinction between soccer as "an objective in itself" and soccer as "an instrument", a means of socialization.

In Italy, 500,000 people from 8-16 years of age play soccer. Of these, only 0.6 per cent become professional and 0.2 per cent make it to the top two divisions, Serie A or Serie B. The challenge of running a Soccer School, D'Ottavio argues, is to ensure that the child who has the rare gift to make it as a pro is identified and can achieve his full potential while at the same time ensuring that the overwhelming majority, those that will never make it, can "improve their relations with society and all those around them, improve their health, their physical development and all-round wellbeing."

Chapter 2

Luigi Agnolin, president of youth and schools soccer at the Italian Soccer Federation

"My dream is that one day people will talk, in a positive way, about the 'Italian school' of soccer."

Anyone who has followed Italian soccer closely over the past 10 years will be aware that while calcio still produces teams with a high level of tactical organization and good technique, and is still capable of providing moments of sublime individual skill from some of the best players in the world, the professional game at club level has been dragged into one crisis after another: fraud, match-fixing, doping, racism and violence have all taken their toll on the image of Italian soccer. The problems came to a dramatic head with the corruption scandal of 2006, in which a number of clubs were investigated for trying to secure favorable decisions from referees.

Many independent observers have blamed the huge influx of money during the 1990s for contaminating the game and politicians have called for a radical overhaul of professional soccer. Others, such as Luigi Agnolin, who was appointed president of youth and schools soccer at the Italian soccer federation in February 2005, believe that change should come from the ground up: a revolution in the way young players are brought up in the game, which puts ethical values firmly at the center of the game.

I spoke to Agnolin in the summer of 2005, before the scandal erupted and in late 2006, after it had died down. In 2005, when asked what state Italian soccer was in, he replied: "When I arrived at the FA, Italian soccer was passing through a crisis. There was no respect for the rules and too many cases of people ducking around obligations and cutting corners. We want to restore respect for the rules. We want soccer to return to its fundamental principles, where athletes confront each other with the proper competitive spirit, not in ways that are sneaky or nasty, or outside the rules."

"We have to recognise that Italian soccer has fallen into a negative vortex from the point of view of behavior and morality; it has broken away from the rules which existed. Our plan is to take soccer back into the realm of established ideas of ethics, rules and behavior."

After a summer of scandal, those observations seemed uncannily prescient. But Agnolin now admits that even he had no idea of the scale of the problems in Italian soccer. "What emerged has reinforced our determination to put ethics and behaviour at the heart of the development of soccer players. It has also been useful in sweeping away some of the doubt which surrounded our initiative. Twelve months ago, not everybody in Italian soccer wanted to hear about these ideas, not everybody believed that they should be a priority. Now it's much easier to talk about them."

Soccer Plus

"We are closer now than we were a year ago to creating a wholly positive identity for Italian soccer. The merit for this goes largely to the Italian national team, not only for their sporting success but for the way the players and staff behaved throughout the World Cup tournament. But I hope that the success in Germany doesn't have a dampening effect on the work being done, with people saying 'we're great at soccer, so what's the problem?'"

"In the first few months after my appointment, we tried to assert the centrality of the youngster, to create the conditions in which he could be natural, joyful and spontaneous but, above all, to have a relationship of naturalness with the rules and with his environment. These were the fundamental principles of the initial phase."

"Then we embarked on an initiative called "Calcio Più" ("Soccer Plus"). We called together all of the representatives of the professional youth teams which had made it to their respective national finals. We wanted to create a situation where we could relate to each other better. We spoke about areas such as diet, the prevention of doping, socialization, motivation, respect for the rules, knowledge of the Laws of the Game – a whole series of issues which come under the banner of 'fair play' had to be asserted. Yes, components of soccer coaching theory, tactics, and technique are important but so are the other aspects which lead to the completeness of the young player in the formative process."

"Then we called representatives of the amateurs and we called managers and those with responsibility for team selection, from the amateurs and also from professional clubs, from clubs like Inter, Roma, Chievo, Milan, Piacenza and Verona. We discussed these issues with them. It was not a case of me imposing anything on them. They themselves brought to light a number of issues through an exchange of ideas and experiences."

"We also met representatives from schools and those involved with the youngest children. This is very important for us because in Italy, in the schools, we are behind other countries. We have to help create the conditions for a type of soccer which is properly formative and not one which is merely a reflection of the professional game. The whole base of soccer doesn't necessarily lead to the world of professional soccer but grass-roots soccer must be based on proper values."

At the heart of Calcio Più is a summer camp in which young players from both amateur and professional soccer benefit from the wisdom and experience of former players and coaches, top fitness instructors, dieticians and many other experts. These old hands don't tell the players about the merits of the 4-4-2 formation or how to spring the offside trap. They talk about sporting values, about fair play, about respect for referees and opponents. They also provide useful advice on a whole range of subjects from the dangers of doping and the importance of diet, to dealing with agents and handling the pressures of modern soccer.

By 2006, in only its second summer, Calcio Più – which Agnolin defines as "a moment of real questioning of everything we know about soccer" – had expanded to comprise 15 summer camps across three venues. The youngsters who attend are chosen not just on the basis of their soccer skills. Disciplinary records at their clubs and performance at school are also taken into consideration. At the camps, they combine classroom sessions with a wide range of outdoor activities which put the emphasis on reliability and leadership.

Other changes for the 2006-07 season included the introduction of a 'green card' for referees, along with the usual yellow and red cards, which can be shown to a young player for a particularly sporting gesture and the promotion of small-sided games up to U13 level to shift the focus away from team tactics and on to individual technique and behaviour. The federation is also talking to physical education experts in order to create a new qualification for a 'sports educator'. The figure would be someone who was well-versed in areas like motor-skills development and learning skills but who wouldn't have to possess the technical and tactical knowledge from a career spent in professional soccer.

Professional advice

Ex-professionals do, however, play a vital role in Agnolin's programme. Luca Marchegiani, the former Lazio goalkeeper who was part of Italy's 1994 World Cup squad, is one of the many big names to have visited the Calcio Più camps to talk to young players. "A professional who talks to young soccer players is likely to get their attention because he has achieved something which for them is still a dream," Marchegiani says.

"I didn't go there presuming to 'teach' them anything. I talked about my experience of soccer and some of the problems I had encountered. There was a lot of dialogue, it wasn't a sermon. In telling them the story of my career, I tried to stress what I consider to be real sporting values, which are the basis of the game of soccer. Soccer today, especially in Italy, is about business and spectacle and it's easy for genuine sporting values to be lost amidst all of that. Youngsters start to think about soccer in terms of money and celebrity and that affects the way they behave, both on and off the pitch."

The key message that Marchegiani wanted to get through to the youngsters was: be yourself. "I told them that they shouldn't feel that they have to conform to some kind of false, hyped image of what a soccer player is. Don't try to change your personality or character to become someone you're not. I stressed the importance of family and school, in this respect. This is where you should look for guidance as you pass through those critical years, from 14 to 18, from being a child into being someone who has to take independent decisions."

Marchegiani, too, talks of a "crisis of values" in top-level soccer, arguing that soccer has "to start re-building those values from the base up." In this regard, he says, Calcio Più is a positive initiative. "It is trying to help the players of the future to behave in the way we would like the players of today to behave."

As Agnolin put it, "the image abroad of the Italian player is someone who is a bit sly, a bit underhand, a diver, a cry baby. We want to create the space for a player who is a serious athlete, but correct, well-behaved and ready to handle the impact of dealing with others in a competitive situation, ready to demonstrate his own validity but through a proper knowledge of the Laws of the Game and a respect for the rules, with a cultural development that can sustain this kind of role."

In summer 2005, during the European U17 Championship in Tuscany, representatives from other national federations and from Uefa came together to compare experiences of youth soccer. The meeting should have been an important opportunity to learn from those abroad but was poorly attended by Italian clubs.

"To be honest, I was disappointed by the level of participation of Italian clubs. I expected a good turn-out even from clubs that didn't have players involved in the U17 Championship. Not everything that the Israeli representative says is right for Italian soccer, and not everything that the Swiss or Dutch have to say. But you can always pick up useful pointers which can then be adapted to your own reality. I am convinced that through dialogue and the possibility of learning about and evaluating what others are doing you can help develop the right direction for Italian soccer. People talk about the 'Dutch school' of soccer, or the 'French approach' to youth soccer. My dream is that one day people will also talk, in a positive way, about the 'Italian school' of soccer."

Achieving the goals

There are two main difficulties with such an ambitious plan. On one hand, you have to get the message out to the provinces and thousands of small amateur clubs, and, on the other, you have to get the message to the big financial interests in Serie A where club owners want to win at all costs. Agnolin explains how these problems are being tackled.

"We are advising the 19 regional representatives of youth and schools soccer and amateur soccer. Each one of these has a meeting within the region, with around 20 clubs and local organizations. Then we meet the representatives of three regions at a time. So, for each meeting we are reaching 60 clubs and with six meetings in total we are in touch with them all. The process starts with a guide line given from the center outwards, which then is transferred wider again. The input is provided from the center but comes through first understanding what they want and need, not just imposing things."

"Italy is very varied and for reasons of geography, climate and so on, things don't work the same way in, say, the Alps as they do in another part of the country. People think in different ways. But we have to try to find a logical thread which runs through all of the different situations and realities. It's like having a necklace with a series of pearls, each one different from the other, but held together by the same thread. We at the federation have to be that thread."

"That is how our relationship works with the base. With the apex – professional soccer – it's a bit different. Professional clubs have different objectives from amateur clubs. As a federation, we have to respect that there are different sporting and economic objectives and different needs. However, the ideas regarding the development of the player, the cultural values, those regarding ethics and behavior, and the respect for the rules, must be enshrined within both sets of objectives."

"The whole process will take three years to complete. Calcio Più has 5 stages:
1) Analysis. This stage was finished in December 2005.
2) Guidance stage, where we talk about what changes need to be made. This stage finished at the end of the 2005-06 season.
3) Verification that the changes are working. This will take place during the 2006-07 season.
4) Correction of any problems. This will begin immediately afterwards and will lead to the final stage in 2008.
5) Drawing up of the definitive guidelines.

Agnolin stood down as president in August 2007 but the Calcio Più project continues.

Pass + Overlap

Appendix i

The structure and organization of Italian soccer from U8s to U20s

The Italian soccer federation, the Federazione Italiana Giuoco Calcio (FIGC), is the main organizer of soccer in Italy. Youth soccer at club level, from U8s to U17s, is run directly by the federation, which oversees over 8,500 clubs, with over 46,700 teams and over 726,000 players. There are over 6,824 Soccer Schools nationwide, of which 3,893 are officially recognized by the federation.

At club level, U20s soccer – the bridge between youth soccer and first-team soccer – is run by the professional leagues. Lega Calcio, which is made of up of the top two divisions, Serie A and Serie B, runs the more prestigious U20 'Primavera' championship. The U20 'Berretti' championship is run by Lega Serie C, which comprises the third and fourth professional divisions. Both come under federation control.

Youth soccer is divided into the following age groups[1]:
U8   (known as Piccoli Amici - which means "little friends")
U11   (Pulcini - which literally means "little chicks" but is a word used generally for small children)
U13   (Esordienti - "beginners" or "novices")
U15   (Giovanissimi - "youngsters")
U17   (Allievi - "pupils")

6-12 years
The youngest players, from 6-12, enroll in Soccer Schools, for which the FIGC has three categories: Soccer Schools, Qualified Soccer Schools, and Soccer Centers. The local or regional branch of the federation assesses the level of each club. The federation philosophy is to give young boys and girls a "correct and gradual introduction to the game of soccer."

Every club which provides soccer instruction for children between six and 12 has to publish key extracts from the UN's Charter for Child Rights which lays down that all children involved in sport have the right:

☒ to have fun and play
☒ to play sport
☒ to a safe environment
☒ to be surrounded by trained and competent people
☒ to follow training sessions which are suitable for their abilities
☒ to compare themselves with children who have the same chance of success
☒ to take part in competitions which are suitable for their age group
☒ to practice sport in absolute safety
☒ to adequate rest periods
☒ not to be a champion

To be recognized by the federation a club must also have adequate sporting facilities and equipment, proper hygiene levels, a satisfactory ratio of instructors to children and a club doctor.

Soccer Schools

To be eligible for the title "Qualified", a Soccer School must have been affiliated to the federation for at least two years; have at least one ball per child; at least three small goals, 4m x 2m; run activities for all levels up to the U17s; have at least one instructor for every 20 children; have at least three qualified coaches; for the 6-12-year-olds have at least one instructor with a qualification appropriate to that age group for every thirty children; follow a training program in line with that suggested by the federation; have at least 10 children enrolled in the U8s, at least 14 in the U11s, and at least 18 in the U15s; run an information program with at least five meetings for coaches, parents and administrators; have a collaboration with a psychologist.

The ordinary Soccer Schools need only one year's affiliation, only two qualified coaches and have a bit more leeway, according to local circumstances, regarding the numbers of players required for each age group. The next rung down on the ladder is the Soccer Center, which is expected to run courses up to U15 level and, ideally, have at least one qualified coach. The federation runs local courses designed to help those who have just set up a Soccer Center understand all of the technical and administrative requirements.

All children have to have a medical certificate which declares that they are fit to play sport and the club has to have the appropriate insurance cover. The federation advises Soccer Schools to run courses of at least six months, with the following timings:

166

U8s: 60-minute sessions, twice a week
U11s: 80-minute sessions, twice a week
U13s: 80-minute sessions, ideally three times a week

Characteristics of the activities for different age groups
U8s
The activity for the youngest children must be predominantly of a motor-ludic nature, i.e. based on movement and fun. Games against other clubs should not be purely about matches but must include fun games and technical activities which motivate the children and allow them to learn gradually. There should be no tournaments with official results and league tables.

Matches should take place in small spaces (e.g. 35m x 25m), with small goals. Balls should be a light size 3, ideally made of rubber. The number of players per team should not exceed five (e.g. 3v3, 4v4, or 5v5) and matches should be either two 15-minute halves or three 10-minute periods. As many children as possible should be involved.

Coaches should have the appropriate qualification and have a particular propensity for working with young children. They should understand both the didactic and physical needs of the child.

U11s
The emphasis should still be on fun but the child should also now be learning more about the game. Matches are normally seven-a-side but, according to the local make-up of the clubs, tournaments can sub-divided into those for eight-year-olds, those for nine-year olds and those for ten- and eleven-year-olds. The youngest continue to play with five players per team, the two older groups with seven players (see below). Matches are played on small pitches, with small goals (4m x 2m) and a size 4 ball.

Matches are divided into three periods of 15 minutes each, during which all players listed on the team sheet must play at least one full period in the first two periods; in the third period substitutions can be made at will.

Each team can use a one-minute time-out at some point during the game. In any match, where one team has an advantage over the other of five goals, the opponent can use an extra player until the difference is back down to three goals. Clubs are advised to use older youth players, such as U17s, to referee the games.

Year 1 (8-9): Matches are played with five players per team on small pitches (e.g. 45m x 25m), with small goals (3m x 2m, or 4m x 2m), and small balls (size 3 or 4) made of either rubber or leather.

Year 2 (9-10): Matches are played with six players per team on small pitches (e.g. 50m x 30m), with small goals (4m x 2m, or larger if suitable of the size of the players), and a size 4 ball.

Year 3 (10-11): Matches are played with seven players with a pitch whose maximum size is one half of the pitch, playing from touch line to touch line. Size 4 ball.

U13s

The activity for this age group is defined as being about play and the promotion of the game with a greater emphasis on developing technique. It is also the age group in which the federation places the greatest emphasis on the moral development of the player. The U13 championship is called the "Fair Play Tournament". Progress in the championship is not based purely on sporting results but also taking into consideration factors such as good behavior and sportsmanship and the number of players utilized.

All matches are divided into three periods of 18 minutes. All players on the team sheet must play at least one full period in the first two, with free substitutions allowed in the third period. Teams can call a one-minute time out.

Year 1 (11-12): Matches are played with seven players in a small pitch, which could be one half of the pitch playing from touch-line to touch line. Goals are 5m-6m x 1.8m-2m. Size 4 ball.

Year 2 (12-13): Matches are played with nine players in a small pitch, no larger than 75m x 50m (typically this might be from the edge of one penalty are to the edge of the other, with a width slightly wider than the penalty area.). Goals are 5m-6m x 1.8m-2m. Size 4 ball. Players in this age group progress in the same year to playing 11v11 on small pitches, no bigger than 85m x 55m. Size 4 ball.

U15s

The activity of this age group is defined as being essentially competitive with a greater focus on results but also on behavior on and off the field. It is the first year in which there is a real assessment of the technical-educational learning process of the early childhood years (6-12).

Matches are played in two 30-minute halves. Teams from professional soccer (Serie A, B, and C) play in national leagues, other clubs play in regional or local leagues. Teams composed of 13/14-year-olds and 14/15-year-olds both play 11v11 in a full-sized pitch with a size 5 ball.

U17s

This is the conclusive phase of the youth soccer program. The next step is the U20s, which is the bridge from youth soccer to first-team soccer. It is highly competitive with an emphasis on perfecting technical development. Matches are played in two 40-minute halves, 11v11 in a full-sized pitch with a size five ball.

U20s
Primavera championship
The principal U20 championship is run by the Italian soccer league, Lega Calcio, which is comprised of teams from Serie A and Serie B. All league teams must participate while admission for teams from Serie C is at the discretion of the league.

The teams are divided into four regional leagues from which the top four teams go forward to dispute the league title in a knock-out phase. Players can be between 15 and 19 at the outset of the tournament. Each team is allowed to field two over-age players, with no age limit, during the normal league season. In the knock-out stages, the over-age players can not be over 21.

Berretti championship
A second U20 championship is run by the third and fourth divisions, Lega Serie C. It is also open to clubs from the soccer league and from the semi-professional and amateur Serie D league. The 2005-06 championship featured 118 clubs: 12 from the League; 36 from the third division (C1), 53 from the fourth division (C2) and 17 from Serie D.

[1]The primary source of this information is the annual official communication published by the Italian FA's youth and schools sector. The Italian FA does not use terms like U13, U15 and U17. Instead, it uses names like Esordienti, Giovanissimi and Allievi. In determining the appropriate equivalent for these age groups, this book works on the basis that, for example, an U17 team cannot include players who are already 17 years of age at the beginning of the season but may become 17 during the season.

Appendix ii

The coaches and federation officials[1]

Marcello Lippi played professionally from 1969 to 1982, including spells at Savona, Sampdoria and Pistoiese. His greatest success as a club coach came at Juventus. Between 1994 and 1998, he led the Turin club to three league titles, the Champions League, the Intercontinental Cup, the European Super Cup and the Italian Cup. After a brief spell at Inter, he returned to Juve from 2001 to 2004, winning two more league titles. He was national coach from 2004 to 2006, winning the World Cup in 2006.

The chapter is based on four sources: a one-to-one interview with Lippi in October 2006; a discussion between Lippi and Uefa's technical director, Andy Roxburgh, at Uefa's Course for Coach Educators, in Florence, on the same day; a coaches' conference in Viareggio addressed by Lippi in February 2005; and Lippi's visit to the Bologna branch of the national coaches' association (AIAC) in April 2005.

Pierluigi Casiraghi was a striker who played 44 times for Italy. He played professional football from 1985 until 202 when an injury ended his career. His clubs were: Monza (1985-1989), Juventus (1989-1993), Lazio (1993-1998) and Chelsea (1998-2002). He was appointed as coach of the U21s in July 2006.

Gianfranco Zola was a playmaker who was one of the most naturally gifted, and popular, Italian players of all time. He was voted the best player in the history of English Premier League club Chelsea by the club's fans. His professional playing career lasted from 1984 to 2005, including 35 appearances for Italy. His clubs were: Nuorese (1984-1987), Torres (1987-1989), Napoli (1989-1993), Parma (1993-1996), Chelsea 1996-2003, and Cagliari (2003-2005). He was appointed as technical consultant to Casiraghi in July 2006.

Claudio Gentile played professional soccer from 1971 to 1987 for Arona, Varese, Juventus, Fiorentina, Piacenza and made 71 appearances for Italy, winning the World Cup in 1982. As a Juventus player he was five times Italian league champion, twice Italian Cup winner, a Uefa Cup winner and European Cup Winners' Cup winner.

His first job after retiring as a player was director general of Lecco (1992-1993). In 1998 he was assistant coach for Italy U20s and then coach from 1999-2000. From July 2000 to October 2000 he was assistant coach for the full national side and from October 2000 to July 2006 coached Italy U21s. He coached the U21s to victory in the 2004 European Championship and won a bronze medal with Italy's Olympic soccer team the same year.

Roberto Dujany holds a Diploma from the Physical Education Institute of Turin and has completed the Italian soccer federation course for Fitness Instructors, at the federation's technical center, Coverciano. From 1991 to 1998 he was fitness coach for sports clubs Chatillon St. Vincent and Valle D'Aosta. From 1999 to the present, he has been fitness coach for Italian soccer federation: in 1999 for the U18s at the European Championship; in 2001 for the Italy team at the Mediterranean Games; and in 2003 for the U19s at the European Championship.

Corrado Corradini joined Lazio as a 14-year old in 1958 and played for all youth teams until 1967. He spent the next 10 years playing professional soccer in the third division, Serie C. After taking his first coaching badge, he coached youth teams at Lazio from 1977 to 1987. Between 1987 and 1992 he coached Italy's U15 and U16 teams before returning to Lazio where he coached at all levels for six years, eventually becoming assistant to first team coach, Dino Zoff.

Between 1999 and 2004 he acted as an observer for the federation in preparation for three tournaments: Euro 2000, the 2002 World Cup, and Euro 2004. In 2005, he was the assistant to Paolo Berrettini, Italy U20 coach, at the World Youth Championship in Holland. In July 2005, he was appointed coach of Italy's Women's U19s and assistant to Pietro Ghedin, coach of the senior Women's national team.

Vincenzo Chiarenza spent 10 years a youth player at Juventus, where he won U17 and U20 titles. He spent 15 years as a professional player (1974-1989) in Serie A and Serie B. He started coaching at Juventus in 1990, and has coached at all levels. 2005-06 was his third season with the U20s 'Primavera' team, with whom he has won the league championship, the Coppa Italia and two Viareggio tournaments.

Paolo Nicolato began coaching 18 years ago and has coached all age groups in amateur and semi-professional soccer and in women's soccer. He has been at Chievo for eight years. Previously he coached the U15s and the U17s. 2005-06 was his third season with the U20s.

Claudio Rapacioli began coaching youth-team keepers for Fiorenzuola, in the fourth division (C2) in 1999, becoming the first-team goalkeeping coach the following season. In 2002-03, he became goalkeeping coach at Brescia Calcio, where he has worked with different levels, including the first team. Presently he coaches keepers for two U20 sides, one which plays in the 'Primavera' championship and one which plays in the 'Berretti' championship. He now coaches at Piacenza (Serie B).

Alessio Pala played at all youth levels for Atalanta up to the first team. In the 1980s and 1990s, he played for a number of other teams in Serie B and Serie C. He joined Atalanta's youth set-up 10 years ago, immediately after retiring as a player. The 2004-05 season was his fifth coaching the U17s, after having worked through the younger categories in the previous four years.

Giovanni Vitali, a former amateur player, has spent eight years with Empoli, working with levels from U15s to U20s. He now coaches at Cuoiopelli Cappiano (Serie C).

Massimo Catalfamo played with Serie D team US Milazzo in Sicily, before gaining a Diploma in Physical Education (ISEF) in 2000. He transferred to Bologna, to specialise in sports science. In 2006-07, he started working at Ravenna Calcio as a fitness coach, initially working with the U11s, U15s and U17s. In 2007, he qualified as an Italian soccer federation (FIGC) fitness coach at Coverciano.

Stefano Carobbi had a highly successful career as a player. He was a defender in the great Milan side coached by Arrigo Sacchi in the late 1980s, playing alongside the likes of Marco van Basten, Ruud Gullit, Frankie Rijkaard and Franco Baresi. Around this time he also played for the national team. After Milan, he played two seasons for Fiorentina before ending his playing career at Lecce. Carobbi spent five years coaching in the Soccer School of Pistoia Nord before joining Fiorentina in 2003. He has worked with the U11s and the U13s and this season took over the U15s.

Stefano Piraccini has spent 16 years coaching at Cesena, coaching at all levels.

Michele Borghi coached for seven years at San Felice sul Panaro before joining Bologna. The 2004-05 season was his fifth at Bologna.

Filippo Fabbri played for Parma's youth teams until a cartilage injury ended his career at 18. He worked as an assistant youth coach at the club for two years, 1998-2000, and in the 2004-05 season was in his fifth year as coach of U13s. He now coaches at Rimini (Serie B).

Giuliano Rusca is a graduate in motor science and a qualified Physical Education teacher. Before joining Inter, he coached for two years at Como and for nine years at AC Milan. He has written three successful books on coaching the 6-12 age group and contributes regular articles to soccer magazines.

Massimo De Paoli coaches Inter Milan's U15s. Before joining Inter, he coached youth soccer at Brescia for 13 years. He teaches motor science at the Cattolica University in Milan.

Stefano D'Ottavio played professional soccer in Serie C and now lectures in Exercise Science at the Tor Vergata University in Rome. As head of the technical sector of youth and schools soccer, D'Ottavio has responsibility for the national network of coaches who oversee the country's Soccer Schools and is the coordinator of selection programs and fitness training of national youth teams. He was fitness coach of the Italian U23 team which won the Mediterranean Games of 1997, of the Italian U21 team which won the European Championship in 2000 and of Italy's Olympic soccer team at the 2000 Olympic Games in Sydney. He worked as fitness coach of Inter Milan from 2000-2002 and was responsible for the fitness training of referees of Serie A and Serie B from 1989 to 2000.

Luigi Agnolin was head of marketing for sportswear firm Diadora in 1970. He has owned and run sports facilities like soccer pitches and swimming pools and spent many years as a teacher, both in universities and colleges of higher education. He is perhaps best known as a soccer referee, having refereed two World Cups (1986 and 1990), and one European Cup final. He was a referee in Serie A for 19 seasons. In recent years, he has worked as a sports journalist both for the press and television and was director general of AS Roma, and later managing director of Venezia and then Verona. He was president of the Italian soccer federation's youth and schools sector from 2005 to 2007.

[1]The information was valid at the time the interviews took place, between 2004 and 2008.

Acknowledgements

Coaching Champions is based on interviews over a four-year period with 30 of Italy's top coaches and administrators, who generously gave their time to explain the secrets of their trade and, in most cases, allowed me to observe their training methods at first hand.

Many of these interviews first appeared in the magazine Soccer Coaching International. Part of the interview with Marcello Lippi first appeared in The Independent newspaper. Part of the interview with Claudio Gentile and part of the interview with Luigi Agnolin first appeared in FIFA magazine.

I am enormously grateful to the Italian soccer federation for its assistance and co-operation, in particular to Marcello Lippi, Pierluigi Casiraghi, Gianfranco Zola, Claudio Gentile, Roberto Dujany, Luciano Castellini, Corrado Corradini, Luigi Agnolin and Stefano D'Ottavio. Thanks also to Sergio Di Cesare, Giuseppe Ingrati and Alessandro Salerno of the federation for their help in setting up these interviews.

I would also like to thank the following coaches and heads of youth set-ups from Serie A and Serie B: Camillo De Nicola and Vincenzo Chiarenza (Juventus); Maurizio Costanzi and Paolo Nicolato (Chievo); Claudio Rapacioli (Brescia); Mino Favini and Alessio Pala (Atalanta); Andrea Innocenti and Giovanni Vitali (Empoli); Oscar Tacchi and Massimo Catalfamo (Ravenna); Pantaleo Corvino and Stefano Carobbi (Fiorentina); Roberto Biondi and Franco Piraccini (Cesena); Christian Ferrante and Michele Borghi (Bologna); Gabriele Zamagna and Filippo Fabbri (Parma); Beppe Baresi and Giuliano Rusca (Inter Milan).

Frank Dunne is a soccer writer and amateur soccer coach based in Bologna, Italy.

He writes about Italian soccer for The Independent, FIFA Magazine and FourFourTwo magazine and writes a regular feature on soccer coaching in Italy for the magazine Soccer Coaching International. He has also written about Italian soccer for the Financial Times, World Soccer, TV Sports Markets and SportBusiness International.

He has coached in the Soccer School at San Donato Calcio, Bologna, since September 2000. Born in Manchester in 1961, the author grew up in Old Trafford, close to Manchester United's stadium.

Monday – recovery + tactical

Tuesday – strength training

Wednesday – technical work (*mobility training*)

Thursday – strength training

Friday – short technical session (or, very occasionally, a match.)

Saturday – recovery / free / (rest) (or, occasionally a match)

Sunday – match.